D0984465

The
Poet and
the Fly

Also by Robert Hudson

The Further Adventures of Jack the Giant Killer

The Art of the Almost Said: A Christian Writer's Guide to Writing Poetry

The Monk's Record Player: Thomas Merton, Bob Dylan, and the Perilous Summer of 1966

Kiss the Earth When You Pray: The Father Zosima Poems

Thomas Dekker's Four Birds of Noah's Ark: A Prayer Book from the Time of Shakespeare

The Christian Writer's Manual of Style, 4th Edition

Beyond Belief: What the Martyrs Said to God (with Duane W. H. Arnold)

Companions for the Soul (with Shelley Townsend-Hudson)

Sinners in a Glass Ball: Two Narrative Poems (chapbook)

Making a Poetry Chapbook (chapbook)

Proof or Consequences: Thoughts on Proofreading (chapbook)

The
Poet and
the Fly

Art, Nature,
God, Mortality,
and Other
Elusive Mysteries

Robert Hudson

Broadleaf Books

Minneapolis

For Shelley

The insect fable is the certain promise.

—Dylan Thomas, "Today, This Insect"

Contents

Prologue

It sounds like *zebub*!

Let me tell you about the summer God talked to me.

I was a few weeks shy of my first birthday. I wasn't walking yet. I was seated on the carpet under the wide archway between our dining room and den, facing brightly lit late-afternoon picture windows. Slowly, I became aware of strange specks floating languidly, slantingly, through the sun shafts. Silence. Everything was peaceful, emanating a hazy warmth—something shimmered inside me and outside me. Of course, I had no words then to describe that incandescence, that penetrating radiance, and the words I now have fall resolutely flat.

Although I didn't realize it until decades later, Whoever Is Out There, Whatever Is Transcendent was speaking to me quietly, clearly, in a language I understood, a language no one needs to learn because we all know it already, have always known it. The language of sentience and awareness, of wonderment and presence. It felt as though God and I were exchanging glances—for I believe we were—ecstatic, joyful, mysterious glances. Theologies, religions, scriptures, sermons, creeds, constructs—all these are well and good, but who really needs them when we have dust motes twisting like strands of DNA in sun shafts?

But why would I notice dust motes? They are, after all, as common as dirt. In fact, they *are* dirt. Although nearly invisible, they teem into our lungs with every breath. Each raindrop that falls is a glob of condensation formed around just such a bit of dust, like the irritant grain of sand in a pearl oyster. We may notice these specks on cleaning day, but otherwise they are like those electrons that, according to quantum theory, only leap into existence by virtue of being observed.[1]

And dust, of course, is how we humans leaped into existence, at least if Genesis 3:19 is to be believed: "For dust thou art, and unto dust shalt thou return." Those words are echoed every Ash Wednesday as the priest imposes the ashes on the congregant's forehead: "*Memento, homo, quia pulvis es*" (Remember, human, you are but dust). It is the stuff we are made of, our literal *ground* of being.

But it wasn't just the dust motes that captivated me. It was the illumination. The fact that the sun was irradiating something that was otherwise invisible, like an X-ray of a single moment of existence. We may be made of dust, but we only gather enough substance, enough self-awareness, to say "we are" because a Light shines in us and through us. There is a reason these kinds of experiences are called enlightenment. We are illuminated dust.

As I grew older, I learned I was not alone. Most people I know can recall similar X-rays of reality from their childhood, though these experiences seem to be a favorite province of poets. Consider William Wordsworth:

> There was a time when meadow, grove, and stream
> > The earth, and every common sight
> > > To me did seem
> > > Appareled in celestial light,
> The glory and the freshness of a dream.[2]

Or consider Welsh Metaphysical poet Henry Vaughan, who described his "angel-infancy" as the time when he "felt through all this fleshly dress / Bright shoots of everlastingness."[3]

Restoration cleric and poet Thomas Traherne, the first writer in this collection, gave a name to that feeling: he called it Felicity. He relates his own childhood encounter with dust: "Some things are little on the outside and rough and common—but I remember the time when the dust of the streets was as precious as gold to my infant eyes."[4] Many of his poems and meditations recount his childhood experiences of Felicity:

> How like an angel came I down!
>   How bright are all things here!
> When first among his works I did appear
>   O how their glory me did crown!
> The world resembled his eternity,
>   In which my soul did walk;
> And every thing that I did see
>   Did with me talk.[5]

C. S. Lewis wrote an entire book to explain such moments—all those small, everyday ecstasies that he referred to not as Felicity but as Joy:

> Joy was not a deception. Its visitations were . . . the moments of clearest consciousness we had, when we became aware of our fragmentary and phantasmal nature and ached for that impossible reunion which would annihilate us or that self-contradictory waking which would reveal, not that we had had, but that we *were*, a dream.[6]

For Lewis, as he grew older, those visitations often came through aesthetic experiences, through poetry in particular, arousing in him "an unsatisfied desire which is itself more desirable than any satisfaction."[7]

That's what good poets do. They create in us a desire, a yearning for the ineffable, a longing to experience the illumination we once felt when we were new in the world. Poets do this by raising to the level of mystery those things that the rest of us consider insignificant and paltry, like dust motes, and they draw our attention to things that are so vastly unmistakable that we rarely notice them at all, like air and sunlight. We reexperience the wonder of newness. We embrace, or rather we are embraced by, Felicity.

The poets in this collection are poets of Felicity. Each in their own way shines a light on—and through—one particular, grandly inconsequential creature, the common fly, and in the process illuminates, as the subtitle suggests, some of life's most elusive mysteries. The fly provides a moment of revelation, a window, a shaft of sunlight, and each poem, I believe, is about the poet exchanging glances with God.

We forget, in our air-conditioned dens and climate-controlled offices, how much of human history is bound up with *Musca domestica*—the common housefly. Flies are everywhere. They are one of our great neglected invariables. When Benjamin Franklin wrote to a friend in 1789 that "in this world, nothing can be said to be certain except death and taxes,"[8] he had most certainly forgotten to add flies to his list. They were probably even buzzing around him as he penned that line. Then again, he did not altogether neglect them, for it was Franklin who devised the adage "A spoonful of honey will catch more flies than [a] Gallon of Vinegar."[9]

In the garden of Eden, how could Adam *not* have been the first poet? What more imaginative task could there be than to ponder all the variety of living things and make up inventive, never-before-thought-of names for them? I picture the scene in which God first brings him the flies, swarming excitedly because they are so eager to be named.

"What do you think?" God asks.

Adam squints and studies the tiny creatures zipping elliptical flight paths all around him; then he smiles as he becomes aware of the noise they make.

"*Zebub!*" says Adam in delight (assuming, of course, he speaks biblical Hebrew). "It sounds like *zebub!*"—which is the onomatopoeic word for *fly*. In Hebrew the *b* is soft, so the word sounds almost like *zevuv*. Buzzing.

God must have smiled too.

Much later, aboard the ark, while all the other animals embarked in their trudgingly ordered pairs, the fly alone must have come aboard in its chaotic thousands upon thousands. Where there are animals, there are flies. And floating zoos are no exception.

An ancient Hebrew legend suggests there were no flies in the temple in Jerusalem, which, by way of a curious bilingual pun, may have led to the coining of one of our names for Satan. The Babylonians called one of their chief deities *Beelzebul*, which means "the Lord of the house"—*beel*, or *baal*, meaning "lord" and *zebul* meaning "house." The Hebrew priests may have feared that this could be misinterpreted to mean "the Lord of the temple"—that is, their own temple in Jerusalem—so by substituting a similar sounding Hebrew word *zebub*, "fly," they renamed the pagan deity *Beelzebub*, "Lord of flies," which thereafter became the name of the "anti-god," Satan, who lived outside the temple quarters. Perhaps the name was even a backhanded way for the priests to equate the worshippers of the pagan god with flies swarming around piles of dung.[10]

Flies are seldom found singly in the Hebrew Bible. Most often, as in the plagues, they gather in swarms and prove viciously destructive. What a formidable threat it must have been when God, through Moses, tried to strong-arm Pharaoh into freeing the Hebrew people by threatening him with an infestation of flies, the fourth of the ten promised plagues: "If you do not let my people go," said Moses, "I will send swarms of flies on you and your officials, on your people and into your houses. The houses of the Egyptians will be full of flies; even the ground will be covered with them."[11] This is not as far-fetched as it may sound. Entomologists calculate that more insects inhabit every arable square mile of earth than there are people on the entire planet. More than seven billion bugs per square mile![12]

And the flies would have been responsible for more than just the fourth plague. Most certainly they would have hung around for the next one, when the livestock grew diseased and died. It's reasonable to assume that flies helped spread the disease that caused plague number five in the first place (see figure 1).

Much later, the prophet Isaiah also prophesied that flies would converge in a judgment from God, this time on both

Figure 1. The fourth and fifth plagues of Egypt as shown in a woodcut by Bartholomaeus of Unckel from the Cologne Bible of 1478–79. Note that the flies are anatomically correct: two wings and six legs each.

Judah and its enemies: "And it shall come to pass in that day, that the LORD shall hiss for the fly that is in the uttermost part of the rivers of Egypt, and for the bee that is in the land of Assyria. And they shall come, and shall rest all of them in the desolate valleys, and in the holes of the rocks, and upon all thorns, and upon all bushes."[13]

The idea that God hisses to summon the flies and bees is wildly creepy. Most modern translations render this—with perhaps more precision but less evocativeness—as "the LORD will whistle" for the creatures, as if God would put fingers to lips and call for them as though they were some kind of entomological Labrador retriever. Hissing is far more terrifying.

In the fourteenth century, Dante too summoned flies and stinging insects together to execute a judgment. In the third canto of the *Inferno*, the poet encounters "a sect of cowards displeasing to both God and his enemies," all those who in life were neither evil enough for hell nor righteous enough for purgatory. These "wretches who were never alive," as Dante describes them, are therefore abandoned for eternity just outside the circles of hell, "naked and tormented by large flies and wasps."[14]

Seven centuries after Dante, French existentialist Jean-Paul Sartre appropriated harassing swarms of flies for his play *Les Mouches* (*The Flies*), a grim retelling of the classic Greek myth of Orestes.[15] In the ancient version, Orestes, who had murdered his own mother and her lover in revenge for her murder of Orestes's father, is condemned by the gods to be hounded by the furies—"infernal goddesses," harpies—who constantly torment him. Sartre takes the imaginative leap of reimagining these malevolent deities as flies—biting, maddening, vengeful swarms of them, like legions of Beelzebubs.

Science too has tended to view flies in the plural, though with less dread and more curiosity. The common housefly, which scientists refer to as *Musca domestica*, is only one of thousands upon thousands of species in the order *Diptera*, that is, "two-winged" insects. The housefly is "common" because it is, for much of the world, the most familiar insect of that order; in fact, the odds are nine in ten that the next two-winged bug you meet will be a housefly, although there are also black flies, hover flies, fruit flies, horse flies, crane flies, blow flies, and more. Not even scientists know how many distinct species of *Diptera* exist, though estimates range from thirty thousand to more than three hundred thousand.[16] They are as countless as stars.

According to paleontologists, the first flies appeared on our planet during the Triassic period, about two hundred million years ago, well before the continents drifted apart to their present locations, at a time when solid earth still formed a vast semicircular landmass geologists refer to as Pangaea. This means that, as a species, flies are found on every continent, including Antarctica, and have been on the earth eighty times longer than

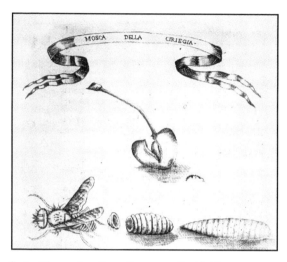

Figure 2. An illustration from Francesco Redi's *Esperienze intorno alla generazione degli'insetti* (*Experiments on the Generation of Insects*, 1668), showing the larval stages of a fly (right to left) observed growing inside a cherry, from the same book in which he describes his experiment with the jars.

humans, who walked—upright—onto the stage of the world a mere 2.5 million years ago.[17]

For most of human history, it was believed that maggots, the larval stage of the fly's life cycle, grew spontaneously out of decaying things. Only 350 years ago did Italian scientist Francesco Redi (1626–1697) disprove the notion of "spontaneous generation" (see figure 2). His experiment was simple. Into each of two jars he placed an inanimate object, in two others he placed dead fish, and in two more he placed pieces of raw beef. Then he covered one jar from each set with gauze, leaving the others open to the air. After a few days, maggots began festering inside the open jars of fish and beef. While no maggots appeared inside any of the covered jars, maggots did appear writhing on the gauze on top of the ones with the meat.[18]

And mother flies are prolific baby makers. A female can lay as many as three thousand eggs in her short lifetime, which can range from twenty to thirty days, depositing her eggs in decaying material or in food (that is, *our* food as often as not). Each laying averages between 75 and 150 eggs, which hatch into squirming little maggots in about a day.

The plagues, Isaiah, Dante, and even Redi's experiment remind us that where there are flies, there is death. The dreaded tsetse fly is one of the top-ten deadliest creatures on earth, killing as many as ten thousand people a year, though that pales in comparison to the one million deaths caused annually by another insect that we often don't think of as a fly, though it is: the mosquito—the world's number-one killer.

Houseflies can carry as many as two million bacteria on their bodies, and various kinds of flies carry such diseases as typhoid,

cholera, scarlet fever and yellow fever, amoebic dysentery, tuber-
culosis, and bubonic plague, to name only a few, which is why
we strive to keep flies, with their bacteria-shod feet and patho-
genic saliva, away from our food. Our custom of praying before
meals began as a way to enlist divine aid in preventing food-
borne illnesses. Once, an Italian friend of mine waved his hand
vigorously over our fettucine to shoo away the flies. "*Faccio la
benedizione*," he said, "I'm blessing the food."

Even our nursery rhymes link flies with death. In "Who
Killed Cock Robin," who but a fly would be the first on the
scene of the bird's demise? "'I,' said the Fly, / 'with my little eye
/ I saw him die.'" And you'll recall that the "little old lady who
swallowed a fly" eventually died as a result.

We'll leave such grim speculations to some of the poets in
this collection, for they will have a lot to say on the subject of
flies and mortality. But they will also have a lot to say about
Felicity and Nature, about creativity and a Creator, about love
and mystery, and about art and grace and life itself, and these
insights are made easier by the fact that these poets, unlike the
biblical writers and the scientists, are nearly unanimous in con-
sidering the fly in the singular.

Writing a poem about a single fly is a romantic notion,
sometimes even an eccentric one, but it opens the door to a curi-
ous kind of empathy, an astonishing act of cross-species identi-
fication. The fly becomes a mirror, as Thomas Traherne asserts,

a clear surface in which to see humanity reflected individually, personally, in contrast to the mass. Even more strangely, in some cases the fly becomes a second self, an alter ego reflecting the poet's own soul.

Like Adam, each of the seven poets in this book has been approached by the Divine and asked to name that nameless thing buzzing in the air. As Emerson once wrote, "The poet is the Namer, the Language-maker, naming things sometimes after their appearance, sometimes after their essence, and giving to every one its own name and not another's."[19]

And with a generous dose of Felicity, this naming leads each poet into a conversation about life's greatest mysteries—a conversation with Whoever Is Out There, Whatever Is Transcendent.

Or as Adam said, "*Zebub*!"

1

Existence
Thomas Traherne

All the world for thee alone doth shine.

When two great religious writers of the stature of C. S. Lewis and Thomas Merton repeatedly recommend the same book to their friends and correspondents, we should pay attention. Lewis declared it to be "almost the most beautiful book . . . in English,"[1] and Merton described its author as "one of the very best and most delightful Anglican writers."[2] That book is the

Centuries of Meditations by seventeenth-century English cleric and poet Thomas Traherne.

Although Traherne wrote his books around the same time that John Milton was composing *Paradise Lost* and *Paradise Regained*, and Antonio Stradivari was building his first violins (that is, the 1660s and early 1670s), the manuscript for the *Centuries of Meditations* was shelved, forgotten, and remained unpublished until 1908—the year that Kenneth Grahame's *Wind in the Willows* was published and Henry Ford rolled his first Model T off the assembly line. By the time Lewis and Merton read Traherne's 240-year-old masterpiece, it had been in print fewer than fifty years and was widely hailed as a major literary find—a classic lost and regained. Even James Joyce twice quotes a phrase from the *Centuries* in his seminal 1922 novel, *Ulysses*.[3]

What Lewis and Merton would have thought of Traherne's meditation on "The Fly" we will never know because that meditation was from another of the poet's lost manuscripts, *The Kingdom of God*, which didn't see the light of print until 1997, three decades after the deaths of Lewis and Merton. Even if the following extract had been the only writing of Traherne's to come down to us, I suspect those two twentieth-century thinkers would still have regarded him as one of the most astonishing visionaries to have written in English.

"The Fly" (from *The Kingdom of God*) by Thomas Traherne

The creation of insects affords us a clear mirror of Almighty Power and Infinite Wisdom with a prospect likewise of Transcendent Goodness. Had but one of those curious and high-stomached flies been created, whose burnished and resplendent bodies are like orient gold or polished steel; whose wings are so strong and whose head so crowned with an imperial tuft, which we often see enthroned upon a leaf, having a pavement of living emerald beneath its feet, there contemplating all the World, that very fly being made alone the spectator and enjoyer of the Universe had been a little but sensible king of Heaven and Earth. Had some angel or pure intelligence been created to consider him, doubtless he would have been amazed at the height of his estate. For all the labors of the Heavens terminate in him, he being the only sensible that was made to enjoy them. The very Heavens had been but a canopy to the insect and the Earth its footstool; the Sun and Moon and stars its attendants, the seas and springs and rivers its refreshments and all the trees and fruits and flowers its repasts and pleasures. There being none other living creature that is corporeal but he, as he had been the center, so had he been the end of the Material World: and perhaps would have seemed worthy of that advancement. The infinite workmanship about his body, the marvelous consistence of his limbs, the most neat and exquisite distinction of his joints, the subtle and imperceptible ducture of his nerves and endowments of his tongue and ears and eyes and nostrils; the stupendous union of his soul and body, the exact and curious symmetry of all his parts, the feeling of his feet and the swiftness of his wings, the vivacity of his quick and active power, the vigor of his resentments, his passions and affections, his inclinations and principles, the imaginations of his brain and the motions of his heart, would make him seem a treasure wherein all wonders were shut up together and that God had done as much in little there as he had done at large in the whole World.[4]

Traherne's inspired fantasy is nothing less than breathtaking. That passage anticipates, by more than a century, the mystical speculations of William Blake, as when Blake asks the tiger, "What immortal hand or eye / Could frame thy fearful symmetry?"[5] So far ahead of his time was Traherne that I suspect you could convince the average college English major that such long, ecstatic declaratives as "the feeling of his feet and the swiftness of his wings, the vivacity of his quick and active power, the vigor of his resentments"[6] were written by Walt Whitman, who lived two hundred years after this obscure English poet-priest. Such phrases as "the stupendous union of his soul and body" and "the exact and curious symmetry of all his parts" are pure *Leaves of Grass*.

Nevertheless, Thomas Traherne was preeminently a man of his own time, which witnessed the upheavals of civil war as well as the full flowering of the scientific revolution.

Born in Hereford, England, in 1637, the son of a shoemaker, Traherne was raised amid the violence of the English Civil War, when the Parliamentarian faction—the "Roundheads" under the command of Puritan Oliver Cromwell—managed to depose the monarchy and wrest control of the government. King Charles I was beheaded when Traherne was eleven years old.

Despite the turmoil, Traherne never viewed his childhood as anything other than a time of joy and wonder, a blissful union with God, though the word he used for that bliss was *Felicity*. It became a major theme in his adult writing, which included both poetry and prose. His collected poems, published more than two centuries after his death, were titled *Poems of Felicity*.

At sixteen, he attended Oxford University. Though officially under the control of the Puritans, the university was known for its Royalist sympathies, so Traherne had little problem being ordained an Anglican priest at the beginning of the Restoration, in 1660, when the monarchy was restored and King Charles II ascended to the throne. Traherne had probably been a Royalist and an Anglican all along, for his hometown of Hereford had been a Royalist stronghold throughout the war.

During Traherne's twenties, from 1657 to 1667, he worked first as rector and then as parish priest in the village of Credenhill, an old Iron-Age fortress town fifteen miles northwest of his birthplace of Hereford. It was in Credenhill, in all likelihood, that he began writing his *Centuries of Meditations* after a woman named Susanna Hopton gave him a blank book in which to record his spiritual insights. He later dedicated the *Centuries* to her and at some point entrusted her with the not-quite-finished notebook; he left most of the fifth "century" (that is, the final set of one hundred meditations) unwritten, most likely for Mrs. Hopton to complete. She wisely did not attempt it, sensing, no doubt, that a spiritual sensibility like Traherne's was inimitable.

After his years at Credenhill, Traherne became the personal chaplain in the household of Sir Orlando Bridgeman, who was the Lord Keeper of the Great Seal of England. Bridgeman's job entailed guarding the matrices for the royal wax seals and attaching those seals to the king's official decrees and documents. Bridgeman relinquished this important post in 1672 after refusing to apply the seals to a document he deemed too lenient toward Catholics. Significantly, at about that time, Bridgeman financed the publication of the only book of Traherne's to be published in the author's lifetime, *The Roman Forgeries*, a critique of the Catholic creeds. Traherne died of smallpox in 1674, at the age of thirty-seven, a year after the book's publication. But *The Roman Forgeries*, with its brisk critical and polemical tone, gave little indication of the stunning mystical insights that its author was capable of.

As a writer, Traherne is often lumped with the Metaphysical poets, which is not entirely apt for he wrote later than most of them, was not as influenced by John Donne, and his syntax and style were not nearly as convoluted—nor as self-consciously clever—as those of the Metaphysicals. His ingenuousness is disarming. Furthermore, his most compelling poetry is often found not in his poems but in his prose. For example, reread his vivid description of the fly when broken into lines as free verse:

> Had but one of those curious
>   and high-stomached flies been created,
> whose burnished and resplendent bodies
>   are like orient gold or polished steel; . . .

which we often see enthroned upon a leaf,
    having a pavement of living emerald beneath its feet,
there contemplating all the World

What Traherne gives us in his meditation on the fly is a thought experiment not unlike those dreamed up by the ancient philosophers, such as Zeno's Paradoxes, and those formulated by modern physicists, such as Einstein's Box and Schrödinger's Cat. For centuries, great thinkers have devised such thought experiments as ways to grapple with new ideas and explore the vast territory between "what if" and "what is."

We'll call this one Traherne's Fly.

Often used in this kind of mental exercise is the technique of testing an idea by pushing it to its most irrational extreme, what is known as a *reductio ad absurdum* (reduction to the absurd). For instance, in his most famous paradox, the ancient Greek philosopher Zeno demonstrates, through seemingly irrefutable logic, that the hero Achilles can never overtake a tortoise in a foot race if the tortoise has been given a head start—because by the time Achilles reaches the tortoise's starting point, the tortoise has moved a little farther on. By the time Achilles reaches that next point, the tortoise has moved a little farther on again, *ad infinitum*. Achilles draws continually closer but can never quite overtake the tortoise. Zeno's point was to demonstrate that things can be infinitely small as well as infinitely large.

Traherne flips this process it on its head by starting with an absurd premise—that a fly is the only living creature—and he follows it to a remarkably rational conclusion. What if, the poet asks, in some alternate version of our universe, a single fly were created as the pinnacle of life, the crown of creation, so that "all the labors of Heaven terminate in him"? What if he were "the end of the material world"? What would follow from that premise?

In a sense, Traherne pursues a sort of *reductio ad gloriam Dei*, "reduction to the glory of God," for Traherne does not see the same thing that the people of his time saw reflected in the fly— that is, an annoying, buzzing insect that hatches out of dead, decaying things (as one writer put it, "The seventeenth century was a great time to be a fly"[7]). Nor does Traherne see the fly as a grim reflection of the human condition—frail, helpless, and transitory—as some of the poets in this collection do. Rather, Traherne looks at the fly and sees the unmistakable glory of God.

Insects, asserts Traherne, are a "clear mirror" in which the power, wisdom, and goodness of the creator are reflected, an assertion that is a sidelong reference to the apostle Paul's famous statement that in this life we "see through a glass, darkly."[8] Some readers assume that Paul is referring to dim windows, but the word *glass* in the King James Version, which Traherne read, refers to a "looking glass," a mirror. In the first century of Paul, mirrors were either highly polished stone or, for the wealthy, reflective metal that had to be regularly polished to prevent tarnishing. Either way, they were "dark" and distorting by modern standards. In the fourteenth century, John Wycliffe translated Paul's line this way: "We see now by a mirror in darkness"[9]—an apt metaphor for all the divine mysteries that Paul felt were obscure, if not impenetrable.

By Traherne's time, polished steel mirrors were common among ordinary folks, although the wealthy could afford mirrors that were more like those we know today, glass backed with thin polished metal. Indeed, Traherne says that the fly's body itself is like "orient gold or polished steel"—itself a mirror. In Traherne's optimistic mind, by extension, all of Nature was a mirror—a *clear* mirror in which the glory of God was brilliantly reflected.

But how could Traherne be so confident about penetrating the mysteries of that glory when Paul—one of the formulators of the Christian faith—was so unsure? The answers, unexpectedly, are science and technology.

Not only had the quality of mirrors improved by Traherne's time, but during his lifetime a major scientific innovation had been introduced: the microscope. When Traherne marvels at the "exquisite distinction" of the fly's legs, the "subtle and imperceptible ducture of his nerves," its "tongue and ears and eyes and nostrils," and "the motions of his heart," he is not anthropomorphizing—imagining that the fly must possess the same basic parts as humans. He is, rather, reporting what the scientists of his time had observed under the magnifying lenses of their microscopes. What they saw was "the exact and curious symmetry of all [the fly's] parts."

In 1665, even while Traherne was writing his meditations, a scientist named Robert Hooke published a phenomenally influential book called *Micrographia: or Some Physiological Descriptions of Minute Bodies Made by Magnifying Glasses*, which included the earliest detailed illustrations of a fly, among other insects, under a microscope (see figure 3). Hooke was literally peering into the unknown. The fly, writes Hooke, "is a very beautiful creature," and after dissecting it, he adds, "nor was the inside of this creature less beautiful than its outside."[10] Hooke's volume was a blockbuster bestseller.

When I first read Traherne's reference to the fly's head being "crowned with an imperial tuft," I thought he was waxing poetic. I had observed flies with the naked eye and had never seen such a tuft. But when I searched online for magnified images of flies, including those from Hooke's *Micrographia*, I saw that Traherne was also being factual. Flies do indeed have fine hairs on their heads between their bulging, multifaceted eyes—a detail made clear under a microscope.

Judging from Traherne's other writings, such as his essay on astronomy in yet another of his posthumously published books, *Commentaries of Heaven* (2007), we know that he was

Figure 3. One of the microscopic images of a fly from Robert Hooke's *Micrographia* (1665).

also fascinated by the recent invention of the telescope. The device had been developed by Dutch astronomers and refined, famously, by Italian scientist Galileo Galilei. That technological advance was about sixty years old when Traherne, referencing Galileo's observations, wrote in his astronomy essay: "Four stars [moons] are lately discovered by the help of telescopes to attend Jupiter and move about it as the moon doth about the earth."[11] So when Traherne writes that his fly's "attendants" are "the Sun and Moon and stars," the awe the poet feels is informed not just by Genesis but by Galileo as well. Not surprisingly, the first

English translation of Galileo's seminal treatise on astronomy, *Dialogue Concerning the Two Chief World Systems*, was published in 1661, when Traherne was twenty-four years old.[12] It too was a scientific bestseller.

It is conceivable that Traherne had even heard about the famous 1668 experiment conducted by Italian scientist Francesco Redi, mentioned in the prologue, who demonstrated that flies do not reproduce by "spontaneous generation" but grow from eggs like every other insect. This knowledge gave Traherne the freedom to ponder with objectivity, and even respect, his own fly's "burnished and resplendent body" and its "quick and active power"—and without the least sense of revulsion. Traherne's fly is a monumental wonder on a par with "the Sun and Moon and stars."

In his own upbeat way, Traherne may have intended his meditation on the fly to be a response to medieval Catholic theologian Thomas Aquinas, who wrote: "Our knowledge is weak to such a point that no philosopher would be able to investigate perfectly the nature of a single fly. Thus one reads that one philosopher spent thirty years in solitude that he might know the nature of a bee."[13] Aquinas's point, like Paul's, was to humble the human intellect, to show the pointlessness of pondering things we are not meant to understand, such as the vast enigma of even a single fly. Traherne, by contrast, argues that the clear "mirrors" of our scientific inventions can inspire us to an ever greater understanding of creation, that these new tools of observation had indeed brought humans, if not perfectly, at least much closer to investigating "the nature of a single fly."[14]

Traherne was also grappling with a philosopher of his own time, Thomas Hobbes, whose materialist philosophy had led some to accuse him of atheism. Hobbes was renowned for advancing a mechanistic view of human interactions, later known as the social contract, and furious intellectual debates about his ideas took place in religious circles at the time Traherne was writing his *Centuries of Meditations* and *Kingdom of God*.[15]

In his influential 1651 book, *Leviathan*, Hobbes argued that without a central government and a strong leader to restrain our human penchant for anarchy and destruction, the "life of man" would be, in his memorable phrase, "solitary, poore, nasty, brutish, and short."[16] The English Civil War had traumatized Hobbes and predisposed him to abhor social chaos, so, in his book, he argued that the great leviathan—that is, a concentrated, unified government—was, for better or worse, our best hope for keeping the most pernicious instincts of humanity in check.

But Traherne rejects Hobbes's pessimism by refusing to consider humans in the mass. God dwells not in the aggregate but in the particular, and to prove this point, Traherne introduces one of the smallest of God's creatures, a single fly, and there finds not chaos but rather divine intention and cosmic wonder—so how much more, Traherne implies, is each individual man and woman a living miracle. A swarm of flies, like humanity, may be anarchic, but a single fly is a marvel. God does not view us as a Hobbesian collective, but as unique creations endowed with a limitless potential for good. Traherne anticipates, by three centuries, G. K. Chesterton's critique of Tolstoy's philosophy of universal love: "Christ did not love humanity; He never said He loved humanity; He loved men. Neither He nor anyone else can love humanity; it is like loving a gigantic centipede."[17]

Elsewhere in his writing, Traherne widens this capacity for wonder to just about every created thing. In his *Commentaries of Heaven*, for instance, he refers to the ant as "a feeble creature made to be an ornament of the magnificent universe, and no less a monument of eternal love. . . . Its limbs and members are as miraculous as those of a lion or tiger,"[18] which again brings to mind the "fearful symmetry" of William Blake's tiger.

So wide is Traherne's capacity for wonder that it encompasses even the invisible, for he could find God reflected in a single atom. In the seventeenth century, the word *atom* was used in the same abstract sense as it was used by the Greek philosophers, to mean the smallest particle of matter, the existence of which was as yet unproven though universally assumed. And yet, in his essay "The Atom" in *Commentaries of Heaven*, using language that seems to anticipate the discoveries of the particle physicists of our own time, Traherne wrote:

An atom is a marvelous effect of almighty power, or a great miracle in a little room; perhaps I may say, it is an infinite miracle in no room, for it is so small that it takes up no place at all but fills an indivisible point of space only, yet there is an unsearchable abyss of wonders contained in it; innumerable difficulties, uses, excellencies, and pleasures concentering in its womb . . . the clear knowledge of which will make us expert in the chiefest mysteries of God and Nature.[19]

Only a prophetic mind like Traherne's could postulate the existence of things dwelling *inside* the indivisible atom—or, in his beautiful phrase, "concentering in its womb"—centuries before atomic scientists themselves could prove that the atom was indeed divisible and could create "difficulties" (nuclear weapons) and "excellencies" (nuclear energy). And how could Traherne have foreseen that humans would one day explore the interior of the atom and find that it was indeed one of the "chiefest mysteries of God and Nature"?

There is also a marvelous playfulness here. Traherne knew that his readers would find his thought experiment about the fly ridiculous, a *reductio ad absurdum*. Then, as now, people assumed that God had created the universe with humans as the obvious, ultimate end in view. Hadn't the writer of the book of Hebrews assured us: "What is man, that thou [God] art mindful of him?

or the son of man that thou visitest him? Thou madest him a little lower than the angels; thou crownedst him with glory and honour, and didst set him over the works of thy hands"?[20] Flies are lowly, negligible even, but Traherne's fly, in its own minuscule way, is crowned not only with "an imperial tuft" but with every bit as much glory and honor as any human—because the fly too was created by God. Traherne refers to "the stupendous union of [the fly's] soul and body." Had any poet before Traherne, I wonder, even suggested that a fly had a soul?

At this juncture Traherne becomes one of the most remarkable mystics to have written in English. While his worldview was informed by science, his focus was supernatural—the wonder and divine grandeur that he glimpsed in the mirror of Nature. Unlike some Christians, Traherne did not fear science. All truth, all revelation, he implied, points to a Creator, and in this sense, Traherne was not just a mystic but a *Nature* mystic—someone who, as Blake said, could "see a World in a Grain of Sand / And a Heaven in a Wild Flower."[21]

Just as Traherne discerns the image of God clearly reflected in the fly, he hints that each of us bears that image as well. We too are "treasures wherein all wonders are shut up." When he writes that the fly is "enthroned upon a leaf. . . . The very Heavens had been but a canopy to the insect and the Earth its footstool"—echoing Isaiah 66:1 ("Heaven is my throne, and the earth my footstool")—he is speaking to the estate of each individual and encouraging each reader to perceive their own value as a magnificently created being. Each of us, distinct and unique, is the goal, the height, the purpose of creation. This was one of Traherne's favorite themes.

In the *Centuries of Meditations*, the book that C. S. Lewis and Thomas Merton admired, Traherne writes:

> Souls are God's jewels. Every one of which is worth many worlds. They are his riches because [they are] his image—and mine for that reason. So that I alone am the end of the world. Angels and men being all mine. . . . God only being the Giver, and I the receiver. So that Seneca philosophized rightly when he said, . . . "God gave me alone to all the world, and all the world to me alone." . . .
>
> That all the world is yours, your very senses and the inclinations of your mind declare.[22]

He repeats this idea more succinctly in the verse he attaches to the end of his essay on astronomy, where he writes, addressing the reader: "But all is thine, for all is so Divine / That all the world for thee alone doth shine."[23] Twentieth-century hymn writer Eleanor Farjeon, who was an avid reader of Traherne, echoes this idea in her most famous hymn, "Morning Has Broken":

Mine is the sunlight!
Mine is the morning
Born of the one light
    Eden saw play.[24]

For Traherne, the realization that the world was made exclusively for him leads us back to our childhood Felicity, that blissful sense of oneness with God.

But this is not solipsism or some sort of narcissistic creed. Traherne knew that he was not the sole creature to exist in the way that the fly in his thought experiment exists. Rather, he was stating that humans, as a species, as a Hobbesian mechanistic-corporate collective, are *not* the crown of all creation, the pinnacle of the natural order. He was asserting that each person is that crown; each individual is "a little lower than the angels, . . . crowned with glory and honor." Felicity is not the joyful union of humans with God but the union of each individual with God. And God's very infiniteness means that each individual alone and uniquely belongs to God—and that there is enough of the infinite Divine left over so that every other individual, also uniquely and wholly alone, belongs to God.

Each of us has been given the gift of five senses with which to fathom the wonders of the universe, of the entire world around us, each of us being "the only sensible," as Traherne says, "that was made to enjoy them." And each has been given the gift of awareness and enough spiritual intuition to make us yearn to know the creative force that vibrates within the fly and the ant and the atom. Traherne wrote in his *Centuries*, "Your enjoyment of the world is never right till every morning you awake in Heaven; see yourself in your Father's Palace; and look upon the skies, the earth, and the air as Celestial Joys: having such a revered esteem of all, as if you were among the Angels."[25]

If no human—if not even a single fly—existed to be "the spectator and enjoyer of the Universe," if no living creature was present and alive, then the entire cosmos would be nothing but a meaningless spark, a flash of light in an endless empty room—or, as Traherne says of the atom, the whole lifeless universe would be an infinite miracle in no room at all.

Traherne's final summation is one of the most startling assertions in all of science or literature: that "God had done as much in little there as he had done at large in the whole World." In other words, if God had made no other creature than a single fly, it would still have been a greater miracle than all the rest of the universe put together.

Each of us, in a sense, is Traherne's fly. Each breathing, sentient, pulsating life rivals in magnificence all the galaxies, nebulae, red dwarfs, black holes, and dark matter that exist, for existence itself is the profoundest mystery and the most incomprehensible miracle of all.

2

Mortality
William Oldys

That which weighs us down also lifts us up.

In one swift, erratic flight, our resplendent fly now whisks us from the vast expanses of the universe to the rackety confines of an eighteenth-century pub.

Imagine yourself amid the clatter and hubbub of a late afternoon in London in the summer of 1731. You're strolling west along the cobbled pavement of Fleet Street, the center of the city's vibrant print trade, and, as a literary time traveler, you're hoping to catch a glimpse of poet Alexander Pope, satirist Jonathan Swift, or other members of the infamous Scriblerus Club.[1]

You peek into the mullioned windows of the Bell Tavern, in the shadow of St. Bride's bell tower, but seeing few people inside, you decide to walk a few blocks farther on to Ye Olde Cock Tavern—both establishments are known to attract the writers, scholars, and newspapermen of London. But then, to the right, across the street, you peer down an alley and spot a signboard for Ye Olde Cheshire Cheese, a tavern rumored to have a sunny upper room, strong ale, and a reputation for hosting some of the city's most eminent wits.

Inside, a dozen or so gentlemen are seated along both sides of a broad table, having gathered as they do on most days for a bit of ale and conversation (see figure 4). They chat among themselves, reading snippets aloud from the *Daily Courant*, London's only daily newspaper, as well as from the *Universal Spectator* and the newly founded *Gentleman's Magazine*—and of special interest are the recent obituaries of satirist Ned Ward and novelist Daniel Defoe. The heavy scents of tobacco and kidney pudding fill the air.

Then something happens. One of the men, a bit younger than the rest, rises from his bench. With his cravat loosened and his waistcoat unbuttoned, he raps a spoon on the table and gazes around with an air of mock gravity. He announces that he wishes

Figure 4. "Toddy at Ye Olde Cheshire Cheese," an etching by William Boucher after a painting by Walter Dendy Sadler, 1896. Though this depicts the tavern after Oldys's time, the interior had changed little since then.

to recite a poem he's just devised. "A drinking song," he explains. The company responds with a loud "hear, hear." Then, except for the clack of hooves and carriage wheels on the cobblestones outside, the room grows quiet.

"It's called," he says, "'The Fly . . . an *Anacreontic*'!" The title alone elicits a burst of laughter, and you wonder how many cups this gentleman has already had. Holding his mug aloft as if proposing a toast, he declaims:

Busy, curious, thirsty fly,
Gently drink, and drink as I;
Freely welcome to my cup,
Couldst thou sip, and sip it up;
Make the most of life you may;
Life is short, and wears away.
Just alike, both mine and thine,
Hasten quick to their decline;
Thine's a summer, mine's no more,
Though repeated to threescore;
Threescore summers when they're gone,
Will appear as short as one.[2]

The scene, of course, is fictional. No evidence exists that the poet, whose name was William Oldys, ever read his "Anacreontic" aloud to anyone, let alone in a Fleet Street tavern. Even so, just a few years after the poem was first published, it was set to music by English composer Maurice Greene with the cumbersome title "Song: Made extempore by a gentleman, occasion'd by a fly drinking out of his cup of ale."[3] Since this "gentleman" did in fact frequent those pubs and wrote his poem around that time, the scene is at least plausible.[4]

William Oldys was born in 1696, the illegitimate son of a civil lawyer. After a difficult start in life, losing his inheritance in the infamous South Sea Bubble, he would eventually become a respected bookman, or, as the occupation was more commonly known, an antiquary. He would rub shoulders with some of England's greatest luminaries, discussing Shakespeare with Alexander Pope and laboring side-by-side on a major publishing project with a young Samuel Johnson, decades before Johnson became better known as *Dr. Johnson*.

Despite a stint in debtor's prison, Oldys managed to make a name for himself by writing and compiling some of the era's most important volumes of biography, history, and bibliography, including a survey of the English theater, a number of anthologies, and the massive five-volume Harleian catalogue, which was an annotated bibliography of materials from the library of Edward Harley, Second Earl of Oxford. Oldys was also the first to compile a bibliography of England's much-neglected medieval literature. In appreciation of Oldys's widely praised *Life of Sir Walter Raleigh*, an aristocratic patron not only sprung Oldys from debtor's prison but appointed him to the post of Norroy King-at-Arms, the person in charge of the nation's genealogical and heraldic records. One writer aptly referred to Oldys as the "reader for the Nation."[5] Altogether, a stellar career.

And yet, for all that, Oldys is nearly forgotten today. If he is remembered at all, it is for his one small but widely anthologized poem about the fly.[6]

✦ ✦ ✦

"The Fly: An Anacreontick" first appeared in the maiden issue of a publication called *The Scarborough Miscellany for the Year 1732*, when Oldys was in his mid-thirties. Although the poem was published anonymously, Oldys acknowledged to friends that he was the author,[7] and while he wrote other poetry, "The Fly" was the only poem of his to appear in print in his lifetime.[8]

The first thing that catches the eye is that high-flown word *Anacreontick* (which we now spell without the *k*)—a word bursting with literary associations. The poet's use of the word was meant to be ironic, injecting some cheeky grandiosity into a poem that is, after all, addressed to an insect. But with that word, Oldys name-checked the ancient Greek writer Anacreon, a celebrated court poet of the fifth century BCE who was known for his charming, elegant verses.

This is not to say that Oldys read those verses in the original Greek. Rather, he leaned on the translations of two English poets of the previous century, Sir Thomas Stanley and Abraham Cowley, both of whom were contemporaries of Thomas Traherne's and, like Traherne, are bracketed with the Metaphysical poets. Stanley's collection *Anacreon, Bion, and Moschus with Other Translations* was published in 1651 and was the first to render into English nearly all sixty of the poems then attributed to Anacreon.[9]

Cowley's versions appeared five years later with the decorous title *Anacreontiques: Or Some Copies of Verses Translated Paraphrastically Out of Anacreon*,[10] and the word *paraphrastically* is indicative since Cowley's eleven poems, while as charming and elegant as anything in Anacreon, are equal parts invention and translation. Although Stanley's collection was larger, Cowley's was more influential because he was better known.

Cowley not only coined the term *Anacreontic*, he set forth guidelines for such verse in English. Although the prosody of the Greek originals varies from poem to poem, Cowley's first rule was that an Anacreontic poem should be written in rhyming couplets, with lines of seven or eight syllables and four stressed beats. This rule was refined a few decades later by poet John Philips, who, following Stanley's lead, suggested that the seven-syllable line was a closer approximation of the Greek, and this became the form that Oldys followed.

The second and more inviolable rule was that the subject matter should be wine, love, or living for the moment—preferably all three together. The concept is embodied in the Roman poet Horace's neat phrase *carpe diem*, "seize the day,"[11] though that theme is far older than Horace or Anacreon, and is as old, in fact, as recorded history. Two thousand years before the time of Christ, for instance, the following verse was carved into the wall of an Egyptian pharaoh's tomb: "Make holiday, / Do not weary of it! / Lo, none is allowed to take his goods with him,"[12]—or, in the words of the popular phrase, "You can't take it with you."

The notion of *carpe diem* is found in the book of Ecclesiastes: "A man hath no better thing under the sun, than to eat, and to drink, and to be merry."[13] And it was so dominant a theme in Greek and Roman philosophy that the apostle Paul even referenced it as an oblique argument for the resurrection: "If the dead rise not," he wrote to the Corinthian church, then "let us eat and drink; for to morrow we die."[14]

The theme of seizing the day became a perennial subject in European poetry, from the rowdy medieval drinking songs of the *Carmina Burana* to seventeenth-century English Metaphysical poet Robert Herrick's famous line "Gather ye Rose-buds while ye may, / Old Time is still a flying."[15] The theme continued to be popular throughout the seventeenth and eighteenth centuries and became a significant influence on the Romantic movement in the nineteenth, as in Edward FitzGerald's *Rubaiyat of Omar Khayyam*, for instance. Contemporary popular music couldn't exist without it.

With his fly poem, William Oldys earned his own small but notable place in that enduring literary tradition. His couplet "Make the most of life you may, / Life is short and wears away" is about as crisp an expression of *carpe diem* as can be found anywhere in literature. Oldys's friend Samuel Johnson even translated "The Fly" into classical Latin, and while those two lines

aren't nearly as crisp in Johnson's rendering, they do contain a
direct reference to Horace's famous phrase:

> Tu quamcunque tibi velox indulserit annus,
>   *Carpe diem*, fugit, heu, non revocanda dies![16]
> [Whatever the swiftly flying year bestows on you,
>   *Seize the day*, for it flees and, oh, it cannot be recalled.]

Johnson was well aware of the ancient pedigree of Oldys's fly.

The word *Anacreontick* in itself would have evoked a clear
image in the minds of the patrons of Ye Olde Cheshire Cheese.
Due in large part to Cowley's *Anacreontiques*, Anacreon was pop-
ularly thought of as the embodiment of the jaded poet, lifting
his goblet of wine to Cupid, the god of love, and encouraging
revelry in light of life's transience. Cowley even appended his
paraphrases with a final poem called "Elegie Upon Anacreon,
Who Was Choaked by a Grape-Stone,"[17] written in the voice
of Cupid himself, who lavishly praises Anacreon as "my *Master*,
and my *God*!"[18] Oldys, of course, adds a mordant twist to this by
lifting up not a goblet of wine but a mug of ale and toasting not
Cupid but a housefly.

One of Cowley's paraphrases, "The Grasshopper," may even
have suggested the idea of an alcohol-imbibing bug, for in that
poem Cowley exhorts the grasshopper to sip drops of dew from
the leaves as if they were "the dewey *Mornings*' gentle wine," and
he concludes:

> But when thou'st drunk, and danc'ed, and sung,
> Thy fill, the flowry Leaves among . . .
> Sated with thy *Summer Feast*,
> Thou retir'est to endless *Rest*.[19]

Then again, Oldys may have been inspired by nothing more than a real fly perching on the rim of his mug at Ye Olde Cheshire Cheese. Whatever his inspiration, he was conscious of the deep and venerable history contained in that single word *Anacreontic*. As one biographer elegantly said, Oldys, with his vast reading, loved nothing more than to discover "novelties among old and unremembered things; . . . he had crept among the dark passages of Time, . . . he knew where to feel in the dark."[20]

While the first half of "The Fly" is a flawless expression of *carpe diem*, the second half moves into darker territory. What begins as a drinking song ends as a lament; the whimsical toast becomes a rumination on the brevity of life. Oldys effectively turns the toast back upon himself by trading places with the fly, whose one summer may be short, but no shorter than the poet's own anticipated threescore. The poem is not about the fly at all but about the poet—and by extension, about all of us as well.

Even in the invocation of the fly in the first line, we sense that Oldys is talking about himself. He couldn't have chosen two better adjectives than *busy* and *curious* to describe the life of an antiquary, whose work required the skills of a scholar, a writer, an editor, a librarian, an archivist, an appraiser, and an antiques dealer all rolled into one. Oldys was, in the words of his biographer, "'a prodigy of literary curiosity' [for whom a] single line was the result of many a day of research."[21] And with his mug of ale in hand, he was also *thirsty*. Oldys would work at his scholarly tasks until about two in the afternoon, says his biographer, after which he would slip around to the Bell or Ye Olde Cheshire Cheese for a drink and some camaraderie.[22]

Unlike Traherne, whose interest in the fly was both scientific and mystical, Oldys's was rhetorical. The fly was a device, a clever way to illustrate the swift passing of time—that is, his own time. As an antiquary, Oldys had good reason to be apprehensive in the face of mortality. He would have found a special poignancy in the words of Ecclesiastes, "of making many books, there is no end,"[23] for although Oldys's published works were voluminous, they were scant in comparison to those he never finished—and those he had hardly begun. His posthumous papers were made up of abandoned projects, scattered notes, and piles of diaries that contained references to "work to be done, researches to be made, his feelings, his sorrows, with an infinitude of items, whose loss is to be regretted"[24]—in other words, enough to fill not just threescore summers, but threescore lifetimes.

His use of that word *threescore* is an echo of Psalm 90:10: "The days of our years are threescore years and ten," though Oldys shaved ten years from the biblical span, from seventy to sixty, most likely for reasons of rhyme and scansion. The poet himself, coincidentally, ended up splitting the difference, dying in 1761, in his sixty-fifth year. He left a gloomy epigram, again referencing Psalms, intended for those who after his death would rummage through the jumbled stacks of books and papers in his large personal library—"Fond treasurer of these stores, behold thy fate / In Psalm the thirty-ninth, 6, 7, and 8"[25]—verse 6 being the key: "He heapeth up riches, and knoweth not who shall gather them." After Oldys's death, his books and papers—his riches—were indeed gathered up for quick profits by booksellers, librarians, and wealthy collectors. One summer was more than sufficient to disperse the books he collected over threescore summers.

Although he was in his mid-thirties when he wrote "The Fly," mortality seems to have weighed on him even then. In one of Abraham Cowley's essays—one that Oldys was most likely familiar with—Cowley neatly summarized what all scholars feel when they reflect on the prospect of death: "If once we be thoroughly engaged in the Love of Letters, instead of being wearied with the length of any day, we shall only complain of the shortness of our whole Life."[26]

That is the lament at the heart of "The Fly."

✦ ✦ ✦

Not long after his poem was published, Oldys was hired to compile an itemized catalog of the enormous library of Edward Harley, Second Earl of Oxford. Oldys had spent years cultivating the relationship, even selling Harley portions of his own personal library as a way to curry favor. For an antiquary, such patronage was necessary because only the wealthiest nobles could afford to amass the largest collections of rare books, though more for prestige than scholarly interest. As Oldys commented, the rich can "never rest till they have gathered themselves libraries to doze in; like children, who will not be quiet without lights to sleep by."[27]

After years of frustration, Oldys, along with Samuel Johnson, was hired to do the job, which gave them access to the finest collection in England at the time. They were overwhelmed. Harley's library contained more than twenty thousand items, including illuminated medieval manuscripts, rare incunabula, antique scrolls, and many historically important documents. Among other rarities, the collection contained one of the earliest known copies of Chaucer's *Canterbury Tales*.[28]

Also on those shelves were at least three volumes by the ancient Roman philosopher Seneca, including a Latin edition of his letters and, in English translation, his tragedies and *Morals*. In several chapters of the latter, Seneca reflects on death, dying, and the passing of time, and he says, "The shortness of life, I know, is the common complaint both of fools and philosophers."[29] Whether Oldys ever read those chapters from Seneca or reflected on their relevance to his fly poem we don't know, though it's possible since the man who hired him to do that work, a bookseller named Thomas Osborne who was in the process of purchasing Harley's collection, often complained that Oldys and Johnson spent too much time actually *reading* the books they were supposed to be cataloguing. (Johnson is said to have grown so enraged by the haranguing that he thumped Osborne on the head with one of the heavier volumes and knocked him to the ground.)

But we do know that in his writings, such as his *Life of Sir Walter Raleigh*, Oldys referenced and quoted Seneca. Oldys was certainly familiar with Seneca's most famous essay, "On the Brevity of Life," in which the Roman reflects on the many ways people distract themselves from confronting their mortality, and he is especially hard on scholars—people like Oldys and Johnson sixteen centuries later—calling them "laborious triflers who spend their time on useless literary problems . . . [for instance] what number of rowers Ulysses had, whether the Iliad or the Odyssey was written first."[30]

As bemused as Oldys might have been at the thought of being a "laborious trifler," he would have been comforted by that essay's conclusion. Seneca says that the true philosopher is prepared for death because the philosopher confronts it directly, gazes squarely into its eyes. By making death an object of contemplation, the philosopher lessens its sting. That is what Oldys was attempting to do in his poem about the fly.

Furthermore, writes Seneca, by reading the works of the great thinkers of the past, we deepen our own lives and, in a sense, lengthen them. We add to the present by gleaning from the past. By vicariously experiencing the lives of those now-vanished sages, we insert bits of their lives into our own, or as Seneca says, the philosopher "makes life long by combining all times into one."[31]

So that word *Anacreontic* is neither an affectation nor a joke; it's a key. Though ironic, it's also deeply sincere. By invoking the millennia of thought resonant in that word, Oldys deepened his meditation on the problem of time and mortality. His days were augmented by the authors and books that he loved. Biography, literature, history, bibliography—all those things that filled Oldys's days, rather than shortening his threescore summers, multiplied them. He was, after all, the "reader for the Nation."

Which brings me to my own personal connection to "The Fly."

When I was in the sixth grade, my English teacher, Miss Jaynes, upended my life. She was tall and slender, with an

Audrey Hepburn–style beehive hairdo, and as gentle a soul as ever chalked a blackboard. I don't remember the circumstances, but one day she said wistfully, quietly (whether to the whole class or to me alone I can't recall), "You don't realize it at your age, but the months and years will fly by faster as you get older."

I was stunned. It was a loss of innocence. For the first time I became aware of life speeding by, my own life. Only yesterday, it seemed, I'd been an infant watching the dust motes floating through the sunbeams, and now, how many birthdays and Christmases had flickered by like frames of film! The fact of my own mortality had been reported like breaking news.

Not long after that, I discovered William Oldys. While burrowing through the books in my parents' basement, I found one old and crumbling volume, a poetry anthology from the 1880s. The covers were loose, and the fragile pages smelled of mold, but they cast a spell. I think that was the moment I fell in love with old books. I sensed both a deep connection to the past as well as a melancholy distance from it, a feeling I suspect came over Oldys every time he pulled a rare old volume from Edward Harley's shelves.

And there I found "The Fly." Among the hundreds of poems in that book, it is the only one I still remember.

How strange I now feel, nearly threescore summers later, to be sixty-five, the same age as William Oldys when he died. Although I couldn't articulate it at eleven, I was comforted by that small poem, and that comfort had to do with art, with self-expression, with aesthetics, even with humor. In Oldys, I found someone who understood my anxiety about the brevity of life but had transformed that anxiety into something else—something profound and elegant and beautiful in its own way. While "The Fly" as a poem may not be on a par with, say, William Wordsworth's "Ode on Intimations of Immortality," it nevertheless lightened the load that Miss Jaynes had burdened me with.

The poem taught me an incomparable, paradoxical lesson, which turns out to be a key to nearly all art at all times and in all places: that which weighs us down also lifts us up. It is the key to the Psalms and Dante's *Divine Comedy* and Shakespeare's sonnets and Mozart's *Requiem* and Van Gogh's paintings. It is the lesson that centuries of Japanese poets taught with their countless haiku about cherry blossoms. The Japanese term for it is *mono no aware*, "a sense of beauty intensified by recognition of temporality."[32] I have no doubt that this is why God gave us art—to cope with the mystery of our mortality, to make sense of the fact that each life comes stamped with an expiration date.

Or is mortality itself the gift because it adds such richness to life? The fact of death pushes us to create art and intensifies our awareness of the beauty around us—all to prepare us, perhaps, for heaven.

✦ ✦ ✦

But for art to be art it must be shared; it must have a social component, which brings us back to Ye Olde Cheshire Cheese. The mortal burdens that weigh on our souls are transformed in a manner that blesses other people. *Carpe diem* is not just about drinking and gathering one's rosebuds; it's about relationships—with friends, with thinkers of the past, with those yet unborn. Those relationships add days to our days and years to our years no matter how swiftly they may be flying by.

William Oldys understood this truth, the necessity of conviviality in light of our mortality, perhaps as well as anyone. Among his posthumous papers, he left an epigram that affirms his connection with the readers of his many books and those who, in centuries to come, might even happen upon his little poem about the fly and find comfort as I did. And in the process of writing this epigram, he also manages to pun nicely on his own name:

> In word and *WILL I AM* a friend to you,
> And one friend *OLD IS* worth a hundred new.[33]

3

Imagination
William Blake

As a man is, So he Sees.

Two decades after the death of William Oldys, another antiquary was busy preserving England's cultural past. His name was Joseph Ritson. Scholar and author by profession and controversialist by nature, Ritson often proved to be a nightmare for his publishers. He was known as what was then called a *precisian*, that is, a stickler for perfection, demanding the highest quality design, paper, and presswork for his books, and as a result, they were expensive and often only marginally profitable, if that. In a letter to a friend, he bragged that his books were "not without some merit as an example of the printer's art."[1]

In 1779, he began preparing a three-volume set called *A Select Collection of English Songs* for which he had a clear vision in mind.[2] In addition to the costly musical notation required for the final volume, he insisted on including decorative illustrations in the first two. So he and his printer, the socially progressive publisher Joseph Johnson, commissioned some paintings from an up-and-coming young artist from London's Royal Academy of Arts by the name of Thomas Stothard.[3]

For printing purposes, of course, such paintings have to be engraved, a meticulous process that requires an engraver to copy each painting by incising fine lines into a thin sheet of copper with small, sharp tools, called burins. When the plate is inked and the surface wiped clean, the ink remains in the tiny grooves; then, when the plate is run through the rollers of an engraving press, the ink is transferred to the paper. Though the image is reproduced in black and white, the engraver can achieve a surprising range of tones and shades with fine cross-hatching and stippling.[4] If written text also appears on a page with an engraving, then that page has to be printed twice: first for the text, then for the image.

To engrave the plates for *English Songs*, Ritson and Johnson hired a friend of Stothard's from the Royal Academy, someone who had recently hung out his shingle as a professional engraver.

The young man's name was William Blake.

Although Blake is now remembered as perhaps the world's greatest visionary artist, he made his living, meager as it was, by laboring as a jobbing engraver for London's publishers. Broader recognition only came decades after his death. When he died in 1827, in his sixty-ninth year, he was too poor to be buried in any but a common grave, the precise location of which was, until recently, a mystery—which is fitting for someone who was never really of this world to begin with, or, as his wife, Catherine, once told a friend in Blake's later years, "I have very little of Mr. Blake's company; he is always in Paradise."[5]

Still, Blake's art and poetry did not go entirely unnoticed. Of those who did notice, many dismissed him as a lunatic, dubbing him "Mad Billy Blake," while others, like critic William Hazlitt and essayist Charles Lamb, were awed, if a bit baffled, by his uncompromising and often impenetrable originality. "Blake began and ended in Blake," wrote American poet Walt Whitman nearly a century later.[6]

Blake wrote and printed his own long, wildly prophetic—and often incomprehensible—poems, which he illustrated with dramatic Michelangelesque human figures. He then colored the pages by hand and bound them into books that only a few collectors had the foresight to purchase. Scholars now refer to them as his "illuminated books," and all told, he produced fewer than 300 hand-printed, hand-colored copies in his lifetime, of which only 168 still exist. They are rarer than copies of Shakespeare's *First Folio*.[7]

Also among those who noticed was Romantic poet Samuel Taylor Coleridge, who once met Blake and after reading one of the illuminated books declared him to be "a genius." When Coleridge's friend William Wordsworth read Blake's *Songs of Innocence and of Experience* (1794), he qualified Coleridge's assessment, saying that the book was "undoubtedly the production of an *insane* genius," though he added that Blake's insanity was far more interesting "than the sanity of Lord Byron or Walter Scott."[8]

✦ ✦ ✦

Born in 1757, William Blake was the second child of a London hosiery maker. From his earliest years, he was precocious, dreamy, energetic, artistically talented, and most intriguingly, subject to startling visions. Later in life, when he was asked when he began to experience these visions, his wife, Catherine, prompted him, "You know, dear, the first time you saw God was when you were four years old, and He put His head to the window, and set you a-screaming."[9] When he was about nine, Blake informed his parents that on his walk that day he'd seen a tree full of angels with "bright angelic wings bespangling every bough like stars."[10] His father would have whipped him for lying if his mother hadn't intervened.

Still, his parents were supportive of his artistic bent. Unable to afford art school for their son, they apprenticed him at fourteen to one of London's leading engravers, James Basire, who recognized and encouraged the boy's talent. Among other projects, Basire assigned him the task of sketching the effigies and statuary in Westminster Abbey, an assignment that inspired Blake with an intense zeal for Gothic art and religious iconography—though not without encountering apparitions of "Christ and the apostles" in the process.[11]

After completing his seven-year apprenticeship, Blake attended the Royal Academy of Arts as a painter and set himself up as a freelance engraver and sometime illustrator for London's publishers and booksellers, people like Ritson and Johnson. Although the commissions were often uninspiring, they put bread on the table. In later years, whenever money grew scarce in the Blake household, Catherine would place an empty dish in front of Blake at dinner, which was her way of saying that it was time for him to drum up some hackwork among his publishing contacts.[12]

✦ ✦ ✦

Among Blake's earliest commissions as an independent engraver was Ritson's *Select Collection of English Songs* (see figure 5), which was formative in a number of ways. First, Blake had always loved to sing, having devised his own songs since childhood, so the collection's love lyrics, drinking songs, and ballads

Figure 5. William Blake's engraving of one of Stothard's paintings, used at the beginning of the "Drinking Songs" section in Ritson's *Select Collection of English Songs* (1783). Stothard's name appears at the lower left, and Blake's at the lower right. Notice how Stothard's name overprinted the word *Drinking*—an example of how engraved pages had to be printed twice.

delighted him and became a valuable resource for a poet who was even then experimenting with song forms in his poetry.

Second, the project brought Blake into closer contact with commercial book publishing, a process that he was already beginning to find cumbersome, soulless, and unreceptive to the kind of poetry he wanted to write. Living as he did at the beginning of the Industrial Revolution, he felt that poetry and art were increasingly subservient to mass production, that creativity was stifled by commerce, or as Blake later declared: "Poetry Fetter'd, Fetters the Human Race."[13]

While engraving the plates for *English Songs*, Blake had his own brush with traditional authorship. A group of friends funded the publication of his earliest poems, called *Poetical Sketches*, only thirty copies of which were printed. In one, Blake corrected the typographical errors in his own hand. How frustrated he must have been to find that the book's compositor had transformed "the rustling birds of dawn" into "the rustling beds of dawn" and slipped an extra *e* into "the greeen corners of the earth."[14]

Ritson's *English Songs* also brought Blake more deeply into the circle of publisher and bookseller Joseph Johnson, who became a source of income as well as intellectual engagement.[15] Johnson was a one-man clearing house for radical thought in Georgian England, having befriended and published many of the most revolutionary thinkers of the era, such as anarchist philosopher

William Godwin, political activist Thomas Paine, and pioneering feminist Mary Wollstonecraft. Blake rubbed shoulders with a few of them in the years that followed, admired some, and ended up satirizing others, sometimes harshly, in his writings.

Finally, Ritson's collection, published in 1783, inspired Blake in one small, specific way. In the "Drinking Songs" section of the second volume, the nineteenth poem, which bears only the functional title "Song XIX," is none other than William Oldys's poem about the fly. Again it was printed without crediting Oldys as the author, though Ritson added a footnote referencing the title of Maurice Greene's 1740 musical setting: "Made extempore by a Gentleman, occasion'd by a Fly drinking out of his Cup of Ale."[16]

A decade later, Blake remembered that poem while creating his *Songs of Innocence and of Experience*, and he wrote his own small poem about a fly.

"The Fly" (from *Songs of Innocence and of Experience*, 1794) by William Blake

Little Fly,
Thy summer's play
My thoughtless hand
Has brushed away.

Am not I
A fly like thee?
Or art not thou
A man like me?

For I dance
And drink and sing,
Till some blind hand
Shall brush my wing.

If thought is life
And strength & breath,
And the want
Of thought is death,

Then am I
A happy fly
If I live
Or if I die.

Echoes of Oldys's poem are unmistakable here. Both poems share the same rhyme scheme and meter (though Blake splits his lines in half), both take place in summer and deal with mortality, and both begin with a direct address: "Busy, curious, thirsty fly" and "Little Fly."

Although Blake's poem begins in an Anacreontic mode, like Oldys's, Blake's original draft took a startlingly different direction in the second stanza. In his notebook, now archived in the British Library, he followed the opening four lines with "The cut worm / Forgives the plow / And dies in peace / And so do thou"[17]—but he deleted them, possibly uncomfortable with the shift in meter or the suggestion that the worm and the fly die passively, in a state of serene resignation. Perhaps Blake sensed he was letting himself off the hook by assuming that the fly would forgive his "thoughtless hand." (Those lines were not lost, however; Blake recycled "The cut worm forgives the plow" as one of the "Proverbs of Hell" in his book *The Marriage of Heaven and Hell*, written around the same time as "The Fly."[18])

So, having deleted that stanza, he takes another tack: "Am not I / A fly like thee? / Or art not thou / A man like me?" As quickly as that, he performs William Oldys's trick of transforming himself into the fly.

Blake's identification with the fly may also have been suggested by one of his favorite books, *The Wisdom of Angels Concerning Divine Love and Divine Wisdom*, by eighteenth-century Lutheran mystic Emanuel Swedenborg, a copy of which Blake hand-annotated in the margins. Swedenborg was a wellspring for Blake's own idiosyncratic spirituality. In one passage, Swedenborg says that those "who have turned away themselves from thinking of the Divine" become "sensual" and no longer see the natural world around them. They see a swarm of insects, for instance, as nothing but "one obscure thing," not realizing, says Swedenborg, that like humans "every one of these is organized to feel and to move, and therefore that it is endued with Fibres and Vessels, also with a little Heart, Lungs, with Air Vessels, Viscera and Brain"[19]—a reflection reminiscent of Thomas Traherne.

But no sooner does Blake see things from the fly's perspective than he imagines the possibility of some ghastly, inscrutable "blind hand," every bit as thoughtless, hovering over his own head; whether Fate or the Angel of Death or some irrational force sweeping through the universe, the poet doesn't say—only that it will brush his own wing. "As flies to wanton boys are we to the gods," says King Lear in a similar vein. "They kill us for their sport."[20]

Anglican priest and writer James Hervey most likely inspired Blake's image of the "blind hand." In his *Meditations among the Tombs* (1748), Hervey ruminates over the gravestones in a rural cemetery. In one passage, he stands at the grave of a young man and reflects:

He solaced himself with the Prospect of a long, long Series of earthly Satisfactions.—When lo! an unexpected Stroke descends! descends from that mighty Arm, which "overturneth the Mountains by their Roots, and crushes the imaginary Hero *before the Moth*"; as quickly, and more easily, than our Fingers press such a feeble fluttering Insect to Death.[21]

Hervey's book too was a favorite of Blake's, and he referenced Hervey in several of his writings. Sometime in the early 1820s, he even painted a large watercolor on paper called *Epitome of James Hervey's Meditation among the Tombs*, which now hangs in London's Tate Museum.[22]

Notice that Blake never actually says that he killed the fly, though its death is implied in that blind hand that makes it impossible for the fly to "dance / And drink and sing." Blake here is echoing a line from Abraham Cowley's "The Grasshopper": "But, when thou'st drunk, and danc'ed, and sung." Cowley's poem was also included among the "Drinking Songs" in Ritson's collection.[23]

So by the end of the third stanza, Blake, through this act of identification, amplifies the fly's death into an image of existential dread—at which point he makes another unexpected move. In the last two stanzas, wanting to affirm life in the face of impending doom, he suggests that *thought*—not life, but *thought*—is the antithesis of death, the antidote to our mortality. Significantly, he says, "If thought is life / And strength & breath"—not "If life is thought / And strength & breath." After all, it was his "want of thought" that killed the fly, so in a sense the poet is pledging to be more full of thought—more thought*ful*—as his way of affirming life.

✦ ✦ ✦

But Blake also provides a visual context for his poetry. Throughout the *Songs of Innocence and of Experience*, he illustrates his poems in some direct way; a picture of a tiger accompanies "The Tyger" ("Tyger Tyger, burning bright . . .") and a lamb and child accompany "The Lamb" ("Little Lamb who made thee . . .").[24] But "The Fly" is an outlier (see figure 6), for no fly appears in the illustration, which leaves the critics to speculate.[25]

Three figures appear. On the left, a young girl plays a game called shuttlecock. In the middle, a mother, or more likely a nanny, encourages a toddler to walk—forming a trio that some critics see as an image of despondency. They note that the surrounding trees are leafless, perhaps barren, and they suggest that the three figures represent a hopeless cycle of life and death, youth and age. The girl is playing a game that is meant for two people, and the nanny and toddler seem detached and joyless. This is, after all, a poem of *Experience*, not *Innocence*.

Other critics respond that the woman seems quite attentive, while the toddler's open posture expresses hope and security. The bare trees suggest that winter has passed and spring is about to bloom. The point of shuttlecock, which differs from badminton, is for two people to see how long they can keep the feathered birdie aloft, but it was also commonly played solo as a test of skill. In some painted versions of the page, the background clouds are bright and sunlit, more vibrant than many pages in *Songs of Experience*, though in other versions, admittedly, the background is lowering, even lurid. It is also possible that at some point Blake may even have changed his own view about the meaning of the image.

Whatever Blake's intentions, the three figures do, in fact, illustrate something in the poem. The young girl's mind is absorbed in her game, and the nanny is focused on the toddler, who seems to be enjoying everything, living wholly, expectantly in the present. In other words, each character illustrates *thought*.

For Blake, the word *thought* signified something far more active and deliberate than just self-awareness or reflection. It was another word for *imagination*, which the poet himself exemplified in that fanciful leap of identification with the fly in the second stanza. As Blake once wrote, "The Imagination is not a State: it is the Human Existence itself."[27] As he says in "The Fly," it is "life / And strength and breath."

At that time, in the early 1790s, Blake was experiencing his most productive period, creating illuminated books with breathtaking

Figure 6. Blake's "The Fly" from *Songs of Innocence and of Experience* (1794), as it appeared before color was added. One can see how this relief-etched illustration differs from Blake's intaglio engraving in Ritson's *English Songs* (figure 5).[26]

speed. In addition to *Songs of Innocence and of Experience* (1794), he produced *The Book of Thel* (1793), *The Marriage of Heaven and Hell* (1793), *Visions of the Daughters of Albion* (1793),

America a Prophecy (1794), *Europe a Prophecy* (1795), *The Song of Los* (1795), and *There Is No Natural Religion* (1795).

During this period, he began to articulate what might be called his theology of the imagination, the notion that the image of God referred to in Genesis 1:26 ("Let us make man in our image, after our likeness") is the imagination itself. According to Blake, we are like God in our ability to imagine. For Blake, the purest, most perfect expression of that divine image was Jesus, who was "all imagination, and acted from impulse, and not from rules."[28] As unorthodox as that may sound, Blake insisted in a letter to a friend that "I still & shall to Eternity Embrace Christianity, and Adore him who is the Express image of God."[29] In the final decade of his life, he forcefully explained this philosophy in an exhortation entitled "To the Christians" in *Jerusalem: The Emanation of the Giant Albion* (1820), the longest and most ambitious of his illuminated books:

> I know of no other Christianity and of no other Gospel than the liberty both of body & mind to exercise the Divine Arts of Imagination, Imagination, the real & eternal World of which this Vegetable Universe is but a faint shadow, & in which we shall live in our Eternal or Imaginative Bodies when these Vegetable Mortal Bodies are no more. The Apostles knew of no other Gospel. . . . Let every Christian, as much as in him lies, engage

himself openly & publicly before all the World in some Mental pursuit for the Building up of Jerusalem.[30]

In that same book, he described in more lyrical terms what he'd always felt his role was as a poet and painter:

> Trembling I sit day and night, my friends are astonish'd at me.
> Yet they forgive my wanderings, I rest not from my great task!
> To open the Eternal Worlds, to open the immortal Eyes
> Of Man inwards into the Worlds of Thought: into Eternity
> Ever expanding in the Bosom of God. the Human Imagination
> O Saviour pour upon me thy Spirit of meekness & love:
> Annihilate the Selfhood in me, be thou all my life!

Notice that lack of punctuation after "the Human Imagination" so that it flows unimpeded into "O Saviour." Between "the Bosom of God" and "Saviour" lies "the Human imagination."

This zealous faith in the imagination goes a long way toward explaining Blake's visions. In a world pulsating with God's creative energy (or as Blake insisted, "Everything that lives is holy"[31]), Blake trusted that whatever fanciful picture appeared to his mind's eye, whatever interesting objects he saw around him, whatever images and thoughts came to him in his dreams and meditations—all of it was vision, a mystical apperception of eternal Truth. When a friend complained that Blake's work was obscure and needed explanation, Blake responded:

> This World Is a World of imagination & Vision. I see Every thing I paint In This World, but Every body does not see alike. . . . The tree which moves some to tears of joy is in the Eyes of others only a Green thing that stands in the way. . . . But to the Eyes of the Man of Imagination, Nature is Imagination itself. As a man is, So he Sees. . . . To Me This World is all One continued Vision of Fancy and Imagination, & I feel Flatter'd when I am told so.[32]

So, were Blake's visions all in his head? Was he just imagining things? In a sense, yes, he was—though he imagined them in the most powerful, real, and truthful way possible. Given the right sunlight and the proper frame of mind, any of us might find that every tree is filled with angels; and given a deep enough faith, we might discover that every church is haunted by apparitions of Christ and the apostles.

Even his technique of illuminating books came to him in a vision. In 1788, Blake's recently deceased younger brother, Robert, appeared to him and in great detail outlined a previously unthought-of printing process in which moveable type could be dispensed with and both text and image could be printed together, an innovative technical process that would leave creative control in William's hands alone. This was the key that Blake had been searching for since engraving the plates for Ritson's *English Songs* and since writing *Poetical Sketches*.

Robert explained that the pictures and the words could be hand-drawn together on a metal plate with an acid-resistant, varnish-like fluid—actually drawn on as one would apply ink to paper. When the plate is then dipped in acid, the unpainted areas—the negative spaces—are eaten away, leaving the raised lines and letters to receive the ink for printing (see figure 6). This is the opposite of conventional intaglio etching and engraving in which the ink is transferred to the paper from the lowered portions of the plate, from the grooves incised into the metal. This new method, which is still used and referred to as relief etching, was the visionary invention of William Blake—and his late brother, Robert.

In Genesis 1, God imagines the possibility of light flooding the void; then he says, "Let there be . . . ," and immediately the light appears. For Blake, the artist both conceives and executes a work of art in just such an act of creation, for it is no coincidence that the English verb *to conceive* can mean "to imagine," "to create," or "to give birth to." Such is the image of God implanted in all of us, in thought, in the imagination.

✦ ✦ ✦

The flip side of Blake's "thought is life / And strength & breath" is his ominous assertion that "the want / Of thought is death." For him, the way "that leadeth to destruction"[33] was nothing other than a chronic *lack* of imagination, exemplified by the rationalists and empiricists of his time, all those philosophical inheritors of the Enlightenment who viewed humans as the center of the universe and religion as a crutch for the weak. In one of the poems in his notebooks, Blake wrote:

> Mock on, Mock on Voltaire, Rousseau:
> Mock on, Mock on: 'tis all in vain!
> You throw the sand against the wind,
> And the wind blows it back again.[34]

Nor were the philosophers alone in their lack of Divine Imagination. In that same poem, Blake targets two scientists as well: the ancient Greek thinker Democritus and English physicist and mathematician Sir Isaac Newton. While Thomas Traherne believed that science revealed the glory of God, Blake felt that science tended to treat God as irrelevant. Democritus was one of the first to theorize that everything that exists is made up of atoms, and Newton formulated laws of motion that seemed to obviate the need for Divine interaction. So in Blake's mind,

they were reductionists, reducing the world to calculable par-
ticles and principles, eliminating the need for the kind of vision-
ary insight that divinely inspired artists should provide for the
world. In his own prophetic way, Blake sensed that science itself
was becoming a de facto religion. He wrote, "Art is the Tree of
Life. Jesus is God. / Science is the Tree of Death."[35]

Not long after writing "The Fly," Blake printed an emblem-
atic color image of Newton, who is shown seated on a rock,
bent over double to draw with calipers on a scroll lying on the
ground. The great English mathematician, absorbed in his calcu-
lations, points emphatically with his other hand to the triangle
and semicircle he has just inscribed. Newton, Blake seemed to
suggest, had reduced the world to plane geometry.

Another of Blake's foils was religious people of a certain
stripe, those who were just as blind to the inner life of the
imagination as the philosophers or scientists. Pharisaism, self-
righteousness, censoriousness, hypocrisy—all these were com-
mon religious manifestations of "the want / of thought" that
ultimately leads to death. Blake wrote, "Prisons are built with
stones of Law, Brothels with bricks of Religion."[36] In a passage
from "To the Christians," he wrote, "And remember: He who
despises & mocks a Mental Gift in another, calling it pride &
selfishness & sin, mocks Jesus the giver of every Mental Gift."[37]
One can imagine what Blake would have thought of those who

have banned the books of J. R. R. Tolkien, C. S. Lewis, and Madeleine L'Engle for containing wizards and witches. For many Christians, creativity is one step away from heresy.

In an even darker and more sinister illustration used as the frontispiece for his book *Europe a Prophecy*, Blake prefigures his portrait of Newton in an image that is commonly mistaken for a picture of God creating the universe. In it, Urizen, a mythical demigod in Blake's imaginary cosmology, takes the giant calipers of creation and inscribes circles of "thou shalt not" on the heavens and earth. Urizen separates and inhibits, establishes boundaries to keep people from expressing themselves, from using their imaginations, from having visions. His job is to impose restrictive laws and limit the scope of creative possibilities. Blake felt that such strictures not only made spiritual abusers and moral authoritarians out of the rule makers but murdered the image of God within us. "In every ban," wrote Blake, "The mind-forg'd manacles I hear."[38]

But the point of "The Fly" is that we need not be bound by such strictures. "Lack / Of thought" does not have to define us. By developing our capacity to imagine, by working at creative tasks, we can, along with Blake, exclaim, "Then am I / A happy fly." With characteristic hyperbole—and with a surprising nod to gender inclusion, which was rare at the time—he later wrote, "A Poet, a Painter, a Musician, an Architect: the Man Or Woman who is not one of these is not a Christian."[39]

Blake's faith was unorthodox, to be sure. As Malcolm Muggeridge once declared, "[Blake] said and wrote things calculated to outrage and disconcert fellow Christians."[40] But there is no denying he was a genius.

Still, did William Wordsworth have a point when he qualified Blake as an "insane genius"? What do we make of someone who was so thoroughly possessed by visions that he was called "Mad Billy Blake"? One answer can be found by comparing him to Joseph Ritson—that noted *precisian*, scholar, critic, social reformer, and compiler of *A Select Collection of English Songs*.

Like Blake, Ritson was a man of immense imagination and productivity. Among his many projects was the first major compilation of the Robin Hood ballads. In his socialist zeal, Ritson was the first to suggest that the outlaw and his merry band "stole from the rich and gave to the poor," or as Ritson delicately phrased it, "transfer[ed] the superfluities of the rich to the necessities of the poor; by relieving the oppressed, and even, when necessary, destroying the oppressor."[41] Though rooted in the old ballads, the Robin Hood we admire today in our books and movies was in that one important way the invention of Joseph Ritson.

Like Blake, Ritson challenged English complacency wherever he found it, whether in the church (Ritson was an atheist), the government (Ritson was an anarchist), or in the British ruling classes (Ritson was an egalitarian), and like Blake he was a radical who supported the American and French Revolutions. Ritson strenuously advocated social change. With the fervor of a Hebrew prophet, he attempted to reform English spelling and grammar and sought to convert England to vegetarianism. Like Blake, he was idealistic, passionate, visionary, and quixotic.

But unlike Blake, Ritson was mad. Unarguably mad. For much of his life he showed signs of severe emotional instability—what we would now call chronic schizophrenia—and as the years passed, his condition worsened. He became more irascible and unpredictable, and his writing more strident, with the result that his published harangues were derided by the public and critics alike.

Eventually, after a series of strokes, Ritson knew death was near. Like William Oldys, he grieved over his unfinished projects, but unlike Oldys, he took action. He built a bonfire out of his manuscripts—indoors, in his own apartment. Friends who recognized that he was in a critical state intervened and under a doctor's supervision forcibly removed him to a country house where he died two weeks later.

By contrast, on August 12, 1827, William Blake spent his final hours singing hymns and reassuring Catherine that "they would not be parted; he should always be about her to take care of her."[42] Then, according to a friend:

He said he was going to that country he had all his life wished to see, and expressed himself happy, hoping for salvation through Jesus Christ. Just before he died, his countenance became fair, his eyes brightened, and he burst out into singing of the things he saw in heaven. In truth, he died like a saint.[43]

That is how the man who once saw a tree full of angels died—fully persuaded of the truth of heaven, of Jesus, of the spiritual visions that had sustained him since childhood, and fully persuaded of God's image living within him, in his own imagination.

"Does a firm persuasion that a thing is so, make it so?" Blake once asked the prophet Isaiah in one of his visionary conversations.

"All poets believe it does," Isaiah replied, "& in ages of imagination, this firm persuasion removes mountains."[44]

4

Compassion
Kobayashi Issa

where there are flies
there are people
and many Buddhas

Even while William Blake was busy creating his first illuminated books in the early 1790s, a young vagabond poet was wandering through the cities, villages, paddy fields, and mountain passes of Japan, half a world away, learning "the way of haiku" from other practitioners of the craft. Observing everything in his path, he rambled from Edo to Kyoto, from Lake Biwa to Mount Fuji, with a pack on his back and his mind buzzing with images and ideas. His name was Kobayashi Issa.

Like Blake, he was a poetic innovator steeped in the religious ethos of his culture, and he would come to be regarded as one of the country's premier poets. Along with Matsuo Bashō and Yosa Buson, Issa would be revered as the third of the "three pillars" of classical Japanese haiku.

But unlike Blake, he did not write just one fly poem. He wrote more than two hundred. Among the twenty thousand or so haiku that Issa penned, you'll find not only flies but fleas, lice, mosquitos, spiders, locusts, slugs, snails, worms, toads, snakes, and other creatures that until then were seldom mentioned in haiku poems because they were often considered uncouth, not respectable enough for serious poetry. But Issa noticed and loved all the creatures he encountered on his travels, especially the uncouth ones that other poets left unnoticed and unloved. He was a keen observer, a sort of whimsical Buddhist realist.

Modern American poet Robert Bly has gone so far as to declare Issa to be (among other things) the "greatest fly poet in the world,"[1] and one can see why by looking at a small sampling of Issa's fly haiku:

> now we've left the house
> you flies can make love
> all you want

✦

a man and a fly
together they buzz
in an empty room

✦

I swat at a fly
on a bloom and kill
the bloom

✦

fly on my hat
precedes me
into the house

✦

the monk the fly
the mosquito
all pass by

✦

my head no longer bald
flies have come
to frolic there

✦

mouth open wide
the dog at the door
chases flies

✦

flies gathering
what attracts them
to these aged hands[2]

But what could have motivated a rural farm boy in eighteenth-century Japan to take an interest in haiku and become a great poet, to say nothing of a great fly poet?

✦ ✦ ✦

How different Kobayashi Issa's life would have been if his mother hadn't died in 1765, when he was two years old. He might never have become a poet, might not have learned to read and write, and most certainly would not have called himself *Issa*. He was born Kobayashi Yotarō, and only years later, when he began his life as an itinerant poet, becoming, as he said, a "homeless lunatic, now roving in the east, now roaming in the west,"[3] would he adopt the penname *Issa-bo*, "Priest Cup-of-Tea." He later shortened it to just *Issa*, "Cup-of-Tea," which he explained to a friend referred not to the tea itself but to the bubbles that form on the surface when it's stirred, bubbles that vanish almost as soon as they appear—like life itself.

Had his mother lived, he would have grown up as the eldest son of a moderately prosperous family, working on his father's farm, cultivating rice to sell locally and at the markets in Edo. As heir to the business, he would have been a good catch for any of the local women, and he would have raised children who in turn would have continued to farm the family's land. Such was the story of hundreds of young men in the rural village of Kashiwabara, Shinano Province, in central Japan in the 1700s.

But his mother did die, and that loss set in motion a sequence of events that forged who the poet would become. For the next five years he was cared for, and apparently spoiled by, a doting grandmother, who may have encouraged him to read and write and indulged his sensitive, imaginative spirit.

Nevertheless, Issa's childhood came to an abrupt end when he was seven. His father, Yogobei, remarried, and the new wife, named Satsu, was the personification of all those harsh stepmothers in classic fairytales, constantly finding fault with her stepson and berating him for any perceived missteps. When Satsu gave birth to a son two years later, Issa was enlisted as the baby's nursemaid, a role he bitterly resented. Four years later his grandmother, his longtime protector and friend, died.

To keep tensions from boiling over at home, Yogobei sent Issa to the big city of Edo, 150 miles away, a journey of several days. The intention was to have the boy become an apprentice— but he never did. Whether the job fell through or Issa just didn't show up is not clear, but he remained in the city, preferring to live as an unwanted street urchin in Edo to being an unwanted son at home. According to his own account, he lived "like a pitiful bird without its nest. I immediately faced the difficulty of finding a place to sleep. . . . I spent days and months under miserable circumstances . . . until by chance I came to learn the art of humorous country-style *haikai* [linked-verse poetry]."[4]

He had left Kashiwabara as a thirteen-year-old boy without prospects. For the next thirty-seven years, he would make his own way in the world, first by finding whatever work he could, most likely as a scribe, then by attaching himself to one of the prominent poetry circles in Edo, and finally by wandering the countryside, living for days and weeks at a time with the master poets he admired, and later, after becoming a master himself, living with the students who admired him.

◆ ◆ ◆

Although Kobayashi Issa and William Blake were contemporaries, even dying within months of each other, the worlds they inhabited could not have been more different. England was nearing the height of its empire, having extended its trade routes to every corner of the earth. It was an expansionist, colonialist global superpower. By contrast, Japan was a closed society. Today a Boeing 787 can fly from London to Tokyo in half a day, but in 1800 a merchant ship sailing from London to Edo, as Tokyo was then called, would take as long as four or five months. Such voyages were risky as well as infrequent because Japan had closed its ports to most European traders, in part as a way of curbing the influence of Christian missionaries among the island's Buddhist and Shinto population. Despite its isolationist policies—or perhaps because of them—Japan experienced an unprecedented cultural renaissance.

Historians refer to that era as the Edo, or Tokugawa, Period. It began in the first years of the seventeenth century when a wealthy, land-owning military leader—a shogun—named Tokugawa Ieyasu and his son consolidated control over the country's warlords and propped up the imperial dynasty. This initiated an era of relative peace, a *pax Japonica*, which lasted more than two and a half centuries. The period saw the rapid flourishing of Japan's merchant economy, agriculture, infrastructure, and local government bureaucracies, all of which led to the creation of an increasingly educated and prosperous middle class.

Because of the increased leisure that such prosperity afforded, the creation of new forms of entertainment was inevitable. Japan's famed kabuki theater was born at this time, as was a new kind of multilayered woodblock printing, known as *ukiyo-e*, "pictures of the floating world." These vividly colored prints found their most perfect expression in the hands of such artists as Hokusai, a contemporary of Issa's, and the slightly younger Hiroshige, who created the iconic image of "The Great Wave of Kanagawa." Their prints are still highly valued by collectors.

In literature, it was the coming-of-age of *haikai*, the extended linked-verse form of poetry from which haiku developed. Predating the Edo Period, *haikai* began as a sort of intellectual party game, called *renga*, in which a group of poets and would-be poets would gather to create verses in a loosely related sequence, as a collaborative exercise of wit. A designated guest would write the opening verse, a short poem of three phrases totaling seventeen syllables. It was called the *hokku* (starting verse). The host would then write a two-phrase response totaling fourteen syllables, called the *waki*. Other guests would then contribute poems that alternated between the *hokku* and *waki* forms until a predetermined number of verses had been composed.

The *hokku* form had to adhere to strict rules: it had to include a reference to a season of the year (called the *kiga*); it had to juxtapose two disparate notions that somehow resonated with each other in an interesting way, often signaled by a word that marked the separation between the two (the *kira*, or "cutting"), and the three phrases had to be written in five, seven, and five syllables respectively. These phrases are written in a single vertical line in Japanese (see figure 7), though in English, we approximate those phrases by printing them on three horizontal lines—what we now call a haiku.

In the second half of the seventeenth century, poet Matsuo Bashō transformed the highly formalized *haikai* into a major literary genre, one that was capable of expressing profound poetic insights. Although he was a master of the longer linked forms, Bashō is now remembered primarily for having raised the single *hokku*, or haiku, to the level of high art. His greatest work, the classic travel journal *The Narrow Road to the Deep North*,[5] combined prose and poetry (a literary form known as *haibun*) and embodied the intensity of Bashō's observations of the world around him. Unlike many of the poets in the big cities, Bashō lived as a tireless wayfarer who transformed even his most fleeting bursts of sensual perception into poetry—a lifestyle that became known as "the way of haiku."

In the century that followed, Yosa Buson, a brilliant visual artist as well as a poet, continued in Bashō's tradition, wandering the countryside, painting landscapes, and writing poetry that brought an even more refined sensibility to haiku poetry. He created a stylized elegance that few poets since have been able to achieve.

✦ ✦ ✦

Not long after the death of Buson, Kobayashi Issa felt called to the "the way of haiku." In 1791, at the age of twenty-eight, and having adopted Bashō as his spiritual mentor, he set out on what became a series of wide-ranging journeys across central Japan, ramblings that were facilitated by an elaborate scheme of

Figure 7. A self-portrait by lay monk Kobayashi Issa, done in about 1815, when the poet was fifty-one years old. At this time, he had just ended his thirty-seven years of wandering and settled in his childhood village of Kashiwabara.

social networking, eighteenth-century style. He compiled a list of more than two hundred haiku poets in various regions, and for the next two and a half decades he would walk from place to place, visiting these poets, writing linked verse with them, and being introduced to other poets, all the while using Edo as his home base.

Not until he was fifty years old, in 1814, aging and ill with a form of palsy, did Issa return to his native village of Kashiwabara to settle more or less permanently. After years of bitter legal disputes, he was able to wrest half his patrimony from the hands of his stepmother and her son. Although he never gave up wandering completely, still visiting his poet friends from time to time, he managed to live in one half of his late father's house and to farm one half of the land.

That same year, he married a local woman named Kiku, a farmer's daughter who was little more than half his age. Two years later, when she gave birth to a son named Sentarō, Issa was overjoyed. A month later, the infant died. Then, even while Issa was still in the midst of his grieving, he contracted malaria as well as a disfiguring skin disease.

In June of 1818, Kiku gave birth to a second child, a daughter, whom they named Sato, and the poet wrote some of his tenderest haiku about children at this time. A year later, Sato too died. In one haiku, the grief-stricken father wrote:

> there on the trash pile
> a red hair ribbon
> spring rain

Two years later Kiku gave birth a third time. The parents, with a dose of wishful thinking, named their son Ishitarō, "Man of Rock," but their hopes were again dashed when Ishitarō died at three months old. Mourning and still ailing from malaria, Issa soon suffered a stroke that incapacitated him for months.

✦ ✦ ✦

It was at this lowest point in his life, in 1821, while still recovering from this series of tragedies, that Issa wrote one of his most famous haiku:

> don't kill that fly
> see, it's wringing its hands
> and its feet[6]

It's easy to see why this haiku, among the hundreds he wrote at that time, is so beloved. It's concise without being cryptic, pointed without being bitter. It's straightforward but contains layers upon layers of resonance, ranging from pathos to levity, from realism to an almost desperate spiritual angst. It is, above all, an example of how much a master haikuist can pack into a few words—in Japanese it is only eleven words long.

We know the scene takes place in summer because *fly* is a *kiga*, a seasonal word, indicating "summer." We picture the poet sitting in his farmhouse when a distracting fly lands somewhere within reach. Although the first line is a command, Issa is commanding no one but himself. His immediate urge is to kill it, but as a lay Buddhist priest of the Pure Land sect, he reminds himself that killing another living thing is not allowed. The fly too is a sentient being on a journey toward enlightenment, through cycles of birth and rebirth, and killing it would end an innocent life as well as bring bad karma upon the one who killed it. After all, even a fly has a "Buddha nature," or as Issa wrote in another haiku:

> where there are flies
> there are people
> and many Buddhas

In two earlier haiku, both of which anticipate "don't kill that fly," we can see Issa's developing moral conscience about such killings:

> with each fly
> I swat I pray
> to Amida Buddha

flies in the doorway
killed even as they
are praying

In the first, Issa is the one who prays—praying to the Buddha of Mercy to forgive him, hoping that these transgressions, these tiny murders, will not hinder his own journey toward enlightenment. He looks to Amida Buddha for compassion. In the second haiku, he notices, perhaps for the first time, how the flies themselves hold their hands in a posture of prayer, and he regrets having killed them as they prayed.

In "don't kill that fly," what prompts Issa to withhold his "thoughtless hand" is not so much the teachings of Buddha as the fly itself. It's wringing its hands. Not only is this a carefully observed detail of fly behavior, it's a sort of visual pun—the assumption that flies wring their hands because they fret just as people do. And this particular fly is beseeching Issa, praying for mercy in the same way that the poet himself had prayed to Amida Buddha.

But then Issa turns his life-and-death confrontation into a tragicomic kind of jest. So earnest is the fly in its prayer that it wrings not just its hands but its feet as well. This kind of whimsy, almost to the point of wisecracking, is what has endeared Issa to readers for more than two centuries. One could perform a sort of

literary stand-up routine reciting nothing but Issa's comic haiku.
I've seen it done.

> at night he goes out
> then comes back
> the cat's love life

>> the dog tilts his head
>> does he hear
>> earthworms singing?

> look out cricket
> Issa is about
> to roll over

But to see only Issa's humor is to miss the point—and the
poet. Comedy and despair can be flip sides of the same coin, and
this is true for no one more than Issa. As often as not, his humor
intensifies the emotion at the heart of his haiku, which in many
cases is his deep compassion for all living things.

"Don't kill that fly"—the whole haiku—is itself a prayer.
Not only does the fly pray, but the poet is praying as well, beg-
ging Fate or Death or Amida Buddha: "Don't kill my loved ones,
don't kill me, don't allow any of the helpless ones in this world
to suffer." Issa is wringing his own hands because, like Blake, he

sees the close connection between his own "thoughtless hand" and the cosmic "blind hand"; he is aware of the destruction wrought by his own lack of compassion. In just eleven words, he evokes the universal mystery of suffering, pain, and death.

In this haiku and thousands of others, Issa responds to the sufferings of others, both human and animal, with a deep sense of empathy and understanding. He is not just the greatest fly poet in the world; he is, in my opinion, the greatest *compassion* poet in the world.

Compassion often gets short shrift in our society. In the West, we tend to focus more on love. According to Christians, in fact, God *is* love.[7] In the King James Version, the word *love* is used 442 times, whereas the word *compassion* is used only 41, not even a tenth as often. (The stats for the New International Version are similar: *love*, 686; *compassion*, 68—again, less than a tenth.) The disparity feels significant because *love* and *compassion* are not the same.

When a scribe asked Jesus for the greatest commandment, Jesus replied, "Thou shalt love the Lord thy God with all thy heart, and with all thy soul, and with all thy mind, and with all thy strength: this is the first commandment. And the second is like, namely this, Thou shalt love thy neighbour as thyself."[8] But note that the scribe didn't ask Jesus for the greatest attitude or feeling; the scribe asked for the greatest *commandment*. In other words, love is something we are commanded to do; it is an act of the will, a decision we make, a "thou shalt."

But *compassion* is different. It's not an obligation. It is, rather, an act of spontaneous identification, of being moved, deeply and emotionally, by the sufferings of others. The reason that compassion is not among the Ten Commandments is that it cannot be commanded. You either feel it or you don't, and those who never feel it are, quite frankly, sociopaths. While we *work* at love, we *live* compassion. It moves us to action.

Consider: the biblical text doesn't say that the good Samaritan *loved* the Levite who had been left for dead by the roadside. It says that "he had compassion on him."[9] The Gospel writers don't say that Jesus *loved* the multitudes when they brought him their sick or came to him hungry; rather, it says he had compassion for them. He felt compassion for the widow whose son had died and for the man whose child was possessed by a "foul spirit."[10]

Compassion, though, isn't just a feeling; it's an act of the imagination, our natural, nearly involuntary response when we allow ourselves to see life through another person's eyes. This is why William Blake believed that Jesus was the incarnation of the divine imagination—because Jesus wasn't obeying some primal divine command to love. Instead, Jesus could imagine—and feel deeply—the griefs and needs and despairs of others. In that sense, perhaps "God so loved the world that he sent his Son" might be more accurately translated as "God had such compassion for the world that he sent his Son." No one ordered God to send Jesus to earth; God did it because God felt deeply how the earth was suffering from death and sin.

Another difference between *love* and *compassion* is this: *love* most often implies a person-to-person relationship, even if one of those persons is divine. Except for our pets, we tend not to use the word *love* with animals. You don't hear people say they love an individual coyote or an osprey or a pond frog, let alone a fly. But we can feel compassion for even the lowliest of creatures when they're suffering, and if we are fully human, that compassion will come naturally—just like the compassion that Issa felt for the fly: "see, it's wringing its hands / and its feet."

Even as I write this chapter, an article has appeared in the journal *Biological Conservation* with the formidable title "Worldwide Decline of Entomofauna: A Review of Its Drivers" by Francisco Sánchez-Bayo and Kris A. G. Wyckhuys.[11] The article, referenced in *The Atlantic* and *HuffPost*, among other news outlets, drew widespread attention and ignited furious debate. The popular media, with its knack for turning a phrase, characterized the article's findings as warning of the impending "Insect Apocalypse."[12]

The authors reviewed more than seventy studies on insect populations worldwide and concluded that "41% of species are threatened," with the butterfly, moth, bee, wasp, ant, and beetle populations among the most rapidly declining. The primary drivers are pesticides, shrinking habitats, invasive species, and climate change. (Were William Blake alive today, he would be startled to learn from one study that there are now far fewer flies in southern England than there were in his day and that the "blind hand" is in large part a human one.)

The researchers estimated that in the countries surveyed, the overall insect population was decreasing at a rate of about 2.5 percent each year, which, if it were to continue at that rate, would lead to most insects vanishing from the earth in the next hundred years. This would not only mean an insect apocalypse but a human apocalypse as well, because insects are essential to our survival. According to Floyd W. Shockley of the department of entomology at the National Museum of Natural History, insects "are foundational members of the food chain, so animals higher up on the chain—reptiles, fishes, birds and mammals—would also go extinct. . . . An estimated three-fourths of the earth's flowering plants and a third of crop plants depend on animal pollinators, most of which are insects. And organic waste would build up without any insects to help it decompose."[13]

Some scientists dissented, citing the amazing resilience of insects—we've all heard jokes about cockroaches being the sole survivors of a nuclear holocaust. Other scientists believe the article's conclusions are too alarmist. Still, none of them argues that insect populations are *not* declining. Though they may disagree about the rate, they acknowledge that *something* is going on.

Not long after that article was published, an even more alarming document appeared. In May 2019, the United Nations released their groundbreaking three-year study by the Intergovernmental Science-Policy Platform on Biodiversity and Ecosystem Services (IPBES), which has been dubbed "The Extinction Report." Their conclusions are dire. Among their findings are that a quarter of all life on earth is threatened and a million land and ocean species face extinction in the coming century due to human-fueled climate change. It documents in statistical detail the rising ocean levels, the warming of the oceans and the atmosphere, the depletion of wetlands, the dying of the world's coral reefs, and the accelerating loss of biodiversity.[14]

As I read these findings, I found myself wishing—to the point of desperation—that more people could read the haiku of Issa, a poet for whom the death of a single fly was a matter of the most urgent moral concern. As Issa once wrote, "Buddha teaches the essential oneness of humanity and nature,"[15] which is more than a religious platitude—it's a scientific fact. William Blake echoed this idea in his proclamation at the end of *The Marriage of Heaven and Hell*: "Everything that lives is holy." Poets have much to teach us about our current environmental crisis.

The question is whether we can muster enough compassion for our fellow creatures—"all creatures great and small," in the words of the old hymn—to change our habits, whether our compassion for living things can outweigh our dependence on fossil fuels and the powerful moneyed interests behind them. We cannot know what kind of world future generations will live in, but we do know that whatever compassion we can muster for insects and other living creatures is in fact compassion for ourselves, our neighbors, our children, grandchildren, and great-grandchildren. "Inasmuch as ye have done it unto one of the least of these my brethren," said Jesus, "ye have done it unto me."[16]

I like to think that Issa, had he been a Christian, would have paraphrased that verse this way:

> where there are flies
> there are people
> and many Christs

As helpless as we may feel in the face of these dire predictions about our changing climate, I believe Issa himself has the last word. He knew that life is fragile, that disaster can strike unexpectedly, that nothing in this "floating world" is permanent, which is why he called it "a world of dew." But he was not a pessimist. In perhaps his most famous haiku, written at another low point in his life, he wrote:

> this world of dew
> is a world of dew
> and yet . . . and yet

5

The Soul
Emily Dickinson

we both believe and disbelieve a hundred times an Hour

Two old cemeteries. In each stands a weather-beaten gravestone, elaborately carved and tilted at a slight angle, having shifted with the earth over the centuries. Although neglected now by nearly everyone except genealogists, these two markers offer a glimpse into the religious beliefs of early New England, at a time when Puritans, Anglicans, Congregationalists, Quakers, and others were staking competing claims for the souls of ordinary working folks in pre-Revolutionary America.

The first gravestone is found in the Old Burying Ground in Wakefield, Massachusetts. Beneath relief carvings of a winged death's head and an upturned hourglass, these words are inscribed on the gravestone of Rev. Jonathan Pierpont, a graduate of Harvard College, a prominent pastor, and a friend of famed Puritan minister Cotton Mather:

> The Reverend Mr JONATHAN PIERPONT
> Late Pastor of The Church of Christ
> In Redding For The Space of Twenty
> Years Aged 44 Years Who Departed
> This Life The Second Day of June 1709

———

> *A Fruitful Christian And a pastor Who*
> *Did good to all, and lov'd all good to do*
> *A tender Husband and a parent Kind*
> *A Faithful Friend Which Who, oh Who can find*
> *A preacher that a bright Example gave*
> *Of Rules he preached, the Souls of Men to save*
> *A PIERPONT All of this, here leves his dust*
> *And Waits the Resurrection of the Just.*[1]

The other stands a hundred miles to the southwest, in a plot called the Ancient Burial Ground, which is a small tree-shaded oasis behind the First Church of Christ in what is today bustling downtown Hartford, Connecticut. A primitive winged angel's head appears amid the ornate scrollwork of the headstone that stands above the remains of Mrs. Esther Gedney Bull:

> In Memory of Mrs Esther
> The Virtuous Consort
> of Mr Joseph Bull
> who departed this
> Life Sept 24th 1783 in
> the 42d year of her Age

———

> *No more the thought*
> *That fills the mind with woe*
> *No more fond tears*
> *of keen Sensation flow*
> *For while perhaps*
> *The hand of God we moan*
> *She swells the Anthem*
> *At her Fathers Throne*[2]

Both verse epitaphs were written in flawless iambic pentameter with rhyming couplets, and both express sentiments that are at once conventional and heartfelt. But a tension exists between the two, a small but telling dissonance in the assumptions they make. In the first, Reverend Pierpont's soul is sleeping with "the Just" as it "Waits the Resurrection"—a general bodily resurrection of the dead at the Last Judgment—whereas in the second, Mrs. Bull's immaterial soul has already joined the heavenly choir, no body required.[3]

The metaphysical question is this: What happens to the soul when a person dies? Which prompts the more basic question: What exactly *is* a soul? Theologians and philosophers have grappled with those questions for millennia, but few ever grappled with them more intensely or more creatively than a woman living in Amherst, Massachusetts, in the mid-nineteenth century who, decades after her own death, would be recognized as America's greatest poet.[4]

Emily Elizabeth Dickinson was born into a prominent family in Amherst, Massachusetts, in 1830. Her father, Edward Dickinson, was a respected lawyer, a state legislator, and briefly a representative to Congress. Her grandfather, Samuel Fowler

Dickinson, was one of the founders of Amherst College and had built the family's stately Federal-style home, the Homestead, on Main Street, which is where Emily was born. She lived there with her parents, her older brother, Austin, and her younger sister, Lavinia, until she was nine years old, when, for financial reasons, their father decided to move to a new house on West Street, around the corner about three blocks away.

Which is where Emily Dickinson fell in love with death.

Although the West Street house was less grand than the Homestead, built of clapboard rather than brick, it was Dickinson's favorite of the two, even after she moved back to the Homestead fifteen years later. The new house was airy, spacious, and much less crowded, and one of its most intriguing features was its view. The rear windows looked out over the southwest corner of Amherst's West Cemetery, and for a teenage girl enthralled by Edward Young's brooding poem *The Complaint: or, Night-Thoughts on Life, Death, and Immortality*, a poem she loved to quote, what could be more alluring? Who knows how many horse-drawn hearses clattered down West Street or how many black-clad mourners could be glimpsed among the trees behind the house? ("Mourners to and fro / Kept treading – treading," she later wrote in a poem.[5]) It must have been a fascinating place to live, or, as Emily might have quoted from Young's *Complaint*, "This is the desert, this the solitude: / How populous, how vital, is the grave!"[6]

When she was fifteen, in the fall of 1846, another grave-yard captured her imagination while she and her family were vacationing in Boston. One of the highlights of their trip was a visit to Mount Auburn Cemetery just west of the city. "It seems as if nature had formed this spot," she wrote to a friend, "with a distinct idea in view of its being a resting-place for her children, where, wearied and disappointed, they might rest themselves beneath the spreading cypress, and close their eyes 'calmly as to a night's repose, or flowers at set of sun.'"[7]

Of course, such somber predilections were not unusual for a sensitive young woman in the 1840s. The poets of the so-called Graveyard School of the previous century, like Young himself, Thomas Gray, and others, were still popular, and that decade saw the publication of such darkly Romantic works as Nathaniel Hawthorne's story "Rappaccini's Daughter" and Edgar Allan Poe's "The Raven." Edward Dickinson had stocked the family's bookshelves with the English Romantic poets. John Keats and Elizabeth Barrett Browning, both of whom had a penchant for writing about death, were among Emily's favorites.

While still a teenager, Dickinson discovered the Gothic romances of the Brontë sisters (imagine reading *Jane Eyre* and *Wuthering Heights* within months of their first publication!), and not long after that, a friend gave her a copy of Ralph Waldo Emerson's *Poems*, a volume that she cherished for the rest of her life. That book concludes with one of Emerson's most famous poems, "Threnody," a lament for his son who died of scarlet fever in 1842. The final lines offer an elegant epitaph: "House and tenant go to ground, / Lost in God, in Godhead found."[8]

Just as formative were the "singing schools" she attended with her family, which were community events at which popular hymns were taught and sung. At times, these hymns were of the grim, funereal kind, like one of the most familiar, "Windham," which begins, "Broad is the road that leads to death" and "Erwick," which begins, "When the vale of death appears."[9] Such lyrics probably shaped Dickinson's faith less than they informed her poetry, molding its metrical forms and vocabulary, and reinforcing her preoccupation with God, heaven, mortality, and the soul.

When Dickinson was thirty-one, death came to Amherst in a very public way. On March 14, 1862, a young man named Frazer Stearns, a local college student serving in the Union Army, was killed in action at the battle of New Bern, North Carolina. Although the Civil War had been raging for nearly a year, Stearns was Amherst's first casualty, and his death unsettled the quiet community. Dickinson's brother, Austin, a friend of Stearns's, was shaken when their father told them the news. "Austin," she wrote to a friend, "is chilled – by Frazer's murder – He says – his

Brain keeps saying over 'Frazer is killed' – 'Frazer is killed,' just as Father told it – to Him." Stearns was buried in West Cemetery.

A month later, perhaps drawing upon her memories of looking out over that same cemetery as a child, Dickinson explained in a letter why she continued to write poetry in the midst of depression and loss: "I sing, as the Boy does by the Burying Ground – because I am afraid." Although she'd been writing poetry since she was eighteen, the Civil War sparked in her an almost frantic burst of creativity. Of the two thousand poems she wrote in her lifetime, nearly half were composed between 1858 and 1865.

Unlike Whitman, who wrote about the war in epic terms, Dickinson confronted it on a more intimate level as she read the newspapers and heard stories of local sons and fathers who had been killed. Her poem "They dropped like Flakes," for instance, was her agonized response to the lists of war casualties printed in the Amherst newspaper. Although the soldiers "perished in the seamless Grass," she wrote in that poem, "God can summon every face / On his Repealless – List."[10] In another poem from that time, she says, "It feels a shame to be Alive – / When Men so brave – are dead."[11]

And it was during this highly charged time, in the late spring or early summer of 1863, that she wrote one of her most famous poems.

"I heard a Fly buzz — when I died" (from Fascicle 26, 1863) by Emily Dickinson

I heard a Fly buzz – when I died –
The Stillness in the Room
Was like the Stillness in the Air
Between the Heaves of Storm –

The Eyes around – had wrung them dry –
And Breaths were gathering firm
For that last Onset – when the King
Be witnessed – in the Room –

I willed my Keepsakes – Signed away
What portion of me be
Assignable – and then it was
There interposed a Fly –

With Blue – uncertain – stumbling Buzz –
Between the light – and me –
And then the Windows failed – and then
I could not see to see –[12]

The poem is quintessentially Dickinsonian. All of her most distinctive traits are on display: the verbal economy ("Heaves of Storm"), the stunning images ("Blue – uncertain – stumbling Buzz"), the word choice ("interposed" gives me chills), the slant rhymes (like "Room" and "Storm"), and of course, the subject of death. (See figure 8 for a copy of the poem in Dickinson's own hand.)

The verse form itself is one she often used: the first and third lines of each stanza have eight syllables, while the second and fourth lines have six, and the meter is iambic. In traditional hymnody, this is called *common meter* because it is, in fact, the most common metrical form found in hymnals.[13] Such familiar hymns as "Amazing Grace" and "Oh, for a Thousand Tongues" are but two of the hundreds upon hundreds written in this form. In fact, you can sing the words of "I heard a Fly buzz" to the tune of "Amazing Grace."

Among the well-thumbed volumes on the shelves in the Homestead was *The Sabbath Hymn Book: For the Service of Song in the House of the Lord*. Section 13, entitled "Hymns Pertaining to the Human Lot as Mortal," collects those hymns appropriate for funerals and memorial services, and half of them were written in common meter, including such solemn hymns as "When downward to the darksome tomb" and "How still and peaceful is the grave."[14]

While Dickinson often wrote her poems in common meter, the fact that she uses it for "I heard a Fly buzz" gives the poem

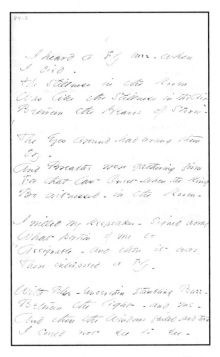

Figure 8. Emily Dickinson's handwritten copy of "I heard a Fly buzz" from Fascicle 26, written in the late spring or summer of 1863. Note her use of short dashes, almost like dots, as punctuation. (Source: The Emily Dickinson Collection, Amherst College Archives & Special Collections. Used with permission.)

an added resonance. By inserting that little fragment of hymn jargon, "when the King / Be witnessed," she tips us off that she is using the hymn form quite intentionally and, with a bit of grim irony perhaps, intends the reader to hear echoes of church music as the poem's narrator lies on her deathbed. The words are intoned as much as they are spoken, giving the poem an unearthly eeriness, as though, in the narrator's not-alive-but-not-yet-in-heaven perspective, she is hearing, vaguely and distantly, the hymns that will be sung at her own funeral.

Dickinson's reference to "Breaths . . . gathering firm / For that last onset" recalls the many hymns in *The Sabbath Hymn Book* that use phrases like "my parting breath," "my last expiring breath," or "my last lab'ring breath."[15]

One hymn in that hymnal even has some uncanny parallels to "I heard a Fly buzz." It's called "Behold, the Western Evening Light," written by a Unitarian minister named William B. O. Peabody. It too is in common meter, and the structure of its narrative is surprisingly similar to Dickinson's. The hymn sets a similar scene: a quiet room in which someone lies dying. "The winds breathe low," says the hymn writer, and "gently flows the parting breath." The "mourners round his bed" wait, as people do "When loved ones breathe their last." Then beyond the window, "a rising star appears," which renews the faith of those "Whose eyes are bathed in tears," and the hymn concludes: "And eyelids that are sealed in death / Shall wake to close no more."[16]

Whether Dickinson had that hymn in mind, we don't know, but the chilling last line of "I heard a Fly buzz" is a sardonic response to all those hymns that portray death as an awakening, an opening of eyes in heaven. For Dickinson, by contrast, "the Windows failed – and then / I could not see to see." Those eleven words are so simple, but few poets are capable of writing a line that gripping. No comforting "rising star" appears in her poem. Just that danged buzzing fly.

Scientists calculate that a fly's wings beat two hundred times per second, three times faster than a hummingbird's, which is what creates its distinctive buzz. On the musical scale, a fly's wings hum an F.[17] Scientists also inform us that when we die, our hearing is the last of our senses to shut down—a fact that elicits an added shiver as we read "I heard a Fly buzz."

Unlike Blake and Issa, Dickinson does not anthropomorphize the fly. She doesn't identify with it or have compassion for it. She doesn't see it as a reflection of God's glory as Traherne does, nor is it a rhetorical device as it is for Oldys. Rather, it's just a thing that's there, a detached phenomenon; it is "other." And its buzz is the sound of alienation.

Once before, she used that image in much the same way. Two years earlier, in a poem that begins "How many times these low feet staggered," she described a housewife whose chores go undone after her death. "The cobweb swings from the ceiling," and "the dull flies" buzz against the "freckled" (unwashed) windows.[18] It is eerie and distancing.

Some critics suggest that the fly in "I heard a Fly buzz" is Death itself or Fate or the Grim Reaper or something akin to Blake's "blind hand." Some argue that "the King" mentioned in the poem is not God or Jesus but Beelzebub, the Lord of Flies. The problem with those interpretations is that Dickinson's fly seems to have no interest in the body lying in the bed. Instead, it's knocking blindly against the window, as flies often do in summer, trying to get out to reach the light. If it's menacing at all, it's because of its remote, stumbling otherness.

Perhaps the fly is not Death so much as it's a sort of cosmic question mark, the embodiment of Dickinson's doubts about what happens after death. While she was raised in an atmosphere of New England Calvinism and inherited much of its gloomy fatalism, she had deep reservations about traditional faith: "Some – keep the Sabbath – going to church," she later wrote, "I – keep it – staying at Home."[19] In one poem, she describes her ambivalence about praying to God because of what she calls "The mingled side / Of his Divinity," that is, the baffling pain God allows to occur.[20] In another poem, she's critical of God for having "hid his rare life / From our gross eyes" while we, at the same time, face "Death's – stiff – stare."[21] In the same letter in which she compared herself to the boy singing by the "Burying Ground," she describes her family this way: "They are religious, except me, and [they] address an eclipse, every morning, whom they call 'their Father.'"[22]

The unflinching horror of "I heard a Fly buzz" is in that image of the fly "interposing" itself between the light and the poet. The tiny insect eclipses the light, just as the relatively small moon can eclipse the entire sun. The fly grows from a speck to a huge shadow that blocks out the windows—"Between the Light – and me." So perhaps the fly *is* God after all, but God as a Divine Eclipse, a black hole.

One thing the narrator in the poem seems sure of is that she cannot imagine *not* being aware of herself. For her, thought is life, as it was for William Blake. Do we even exist apart from our self-awareness? Can we even think about what it would be like *not* to think? In response to the question *What is a soul*, Dickinson's answer is that it's consciousness itself. So the fly may be an image of the self-aware soul, perhaps in its final attempt, battering itself against the window of eternity as it seeks "the King" with its own "Blue – uncertain – stumbling Buzz."

All these interpretations are possible, and Dickinson doesn't drop so much as a hint that any one of them might be more valid than the others. In her indirect way, she has a knack for telling us what it feels like to face the same grim existential questions she faced: What is the soul? *Is* there a soul? What happens to us when we die?

Dickinson's angst about the afterlife—about the fate of the soul itself—was exacerbated by the fact that Christian theology had been split over these issues since the time of Christ, a split exemplified by the two epitaphs quoted at the beginning of this chapter.

Since the first century, some theologians have assumed that the soul dies with the body and either ceases to exist entirely for a time or perhaps slumbers without thought or perception until the general resurrection when it receives a new physical body or the old one reconstituted. This view, promulgated by Martin Luther among others, is called *mortalism*, or, more technically, *thnetopsychism*, and it was the dominant view of most Protestants until the seventeenth century. This was the view of Reverend Jonathan Pierpont's epitaph writer—and of Pierpont himself no doubt—awaiting "the Resurrection of the Just."

Other theologians believed in what was called *particular resurrection*, which means that the individual soul is immortal, existing independently of the body, and is judged by God the instant a person dies. Thereafter, the soul ascends to heaven—like Mrs. Esther Gedney Bull who "swells the Anthems / At her Father's Throne"—or descends to hell or, alternatively, is sent to purgatory according to Roman Catholic theology. Those who espouse *particular resurrection* claim a single biblical proof text: Jesus's parable of Lazarus and the rich man. When Lazarus dies, he is "carried by the angels into Abraham's bosom," whereas when the rich man dies, he ends up "in hell . . . in torments."[23] In either case, the soul lives on, apart from a physical body. This view was modified somewhat by John Calvin, who espoused *conditionalism*—that is, the soul is mortal, but God grants it immortality as soon as a person comes to faith in Christ. The souls of those who do not believe in the redemptive power of Christ simply die—a theory that is called, predictably, *annihilationism.*

No wonder Emily Dickinson, like the boy by the Burying Ground, was "afraid." And no wonder she found little comfort in the church's conventional and often inconsistent answers to her most existential concerns. She lived at a time when the old-style mortalism was giving way to conditional immortalism, and the theological struggle for her was real, complicated by the fact that she was ultimately terrified by, and perhaps resigned to, the possibility of annihilation.

Fortunately for us, she transformed these mortal tensions into immortal poetry. In scores and scores of her poems, she clings predominantly to mortalist concepts of the soul. In "A long – long Sleep," for instance, written in late 1862, she epitomizes, somewhat whimsically, the mortalist view:

> Was ever idleness like This?
> Upon a Bank of Stone
> To bask the Centuries away –
> Nor once look up – for Noon?[24]

Or more pointedly, in one of her most famous poems, "Because I could not stop for Death," she describes how Death stopped its carriage to transport her to "a House that seemed / A Swelling of the Ground." Only later, much later, perhaps at the last judgment, does she realize that

> Since then – 'tis Centuries – and yet
> Feels shorter than the Day
> I first surmised the Horses' Heads
> Were toward Eternity –[25]

(You might also have noticed that both those poems were written in common meter.)

But that soul sleep is an extremely long one in her poems, and seldom does she describe a joyful awakening in heaven, in God's presence. She does, however, often portray the wonders of Nature as God's presence, as heaven on earth—an awakening to the here and now. Occasionally she paints portraits of heaven, as in "I never saw a Moor," written in 1864, but she does so in terms of natural imagery. Although she's never seen the sea or a moor or a hillside blooming with heather, she writes, she is sure that's what heaven will look like:

> I never spoke with God
> Nor visited in Heaven –
> Yes certain am I of the spot
> As if the Checks were given –[26]

In another poem, she describes heaven this way: "No further 'tis, than Here –".[27] For her, heaven is *here* because this is where her conscious mind lives; she seems unsure of what consciousness would be like over *there*, in the heaven of traditional faith. She can picture heaven in her imagination, but she never quite seems to place herself there. This may be due to her own perceived loss of faith. While she believes heaven is real, she doubts whether she will be one of the elect. "'Heaven' – is what I cannot reach!" she writes in one poem, and "Why – do they shut me out of Heaven?" she asks in another.[28]

"I heard a Fly buzz" contains, in one poem, all her fears and doubts. She acknowledges the possibility of being immediately in God's presence, "when the King / Be witnessed – in the Room" (particular resurrection); and the possibility of a "long sleep" when the lights go dark and she "cannot see to see" (mortalism). And then there's that terrifying third possibility—that death is death, that the soul vanishes, and that that fly will be the last thing she ever hears.

✦ ✦ ✦

So what does Dickinson believe? Does she leave the reader comfortless, not knowing whether the soul—her soul and our soul—is destined for heaven or hell or endless nothingness?

In 1882, a few years before her death, she wrote to a friend, "On subjects of which we know nothing, . . . we both believe and disbelieve a hundred times an Hour, which keeps Believing nimble."[29] Although the words were meant to be humorous in the context of the letter, they are nevertheless emblematic of Dickinson's own view of the soul. Scholar James McIntosh refers to this as Dickinson's "nimble believing," which he defines as "Believing for intense moments in a spiritual life without permanently subscribing to any received system of belief."[30]

This is not agnosticism. Dickinson is not refusing to believe until belief is justified to her reason. Rather, she is registering the experience of each living moment in all its potentiality, which leads her—"a hundred times an Hour"—not just to believing and disbelieving *alternately* but also, somehow, *simultaneously*. "Lord, I believe," the possessed child's father said to Jesus, "help thou mine unbelief."[31] Or as Polish poet Czeslaw Milosz wrote more than a century after Dickinson, "Treat with understanding persons of weak faith. / Myself included. One day I believe, another I disbelieve."[32]

In her poem, Dickinson is not seeking conventional assurances about what happens after death. As she says, she has already "Signed away / What portion of me be / Assignable," leaving nothing but her stark, unassignable, conscious awareness of that buzzing fly, and she holds that moment out to us, her readers, in all its terrible inscrutability.

Some readers claim that Dickinson is difficult to understand, too cryptic and multilayered, but perhaps the word *honest* is more apt. She articulates with utter authenticity the actual lived experience of many people I know—and my own as well—in that we daily find ourselves living with both hope and doubt at the same moment, with certainty and skepticism, confidence and anxiety, belief and disbelief. This is why, I suspect, she is so beloved. She understands the wrenching ambiguities we live with. As she wrote in one poem, "This timid life of Evidence / Keeps pleading – 'I don't know.'"[33] She knows that all of us daily dwell with the eternal, impenetrable mystery of the soul as if it were a fly buzzing against the window.

✦ ✦ ✦

In 1886, sensing her own death approaching, Dickinson wrote a note to her cousins Louise and Frances Norcross, of whom she was especially fond:

> Little cousins,
> Called back.
> Emily.[34]

While *Called Back* was the title of a mystery novel she had read the year before, those words had a resonance for another reason and suggest a further possibility for the soul after death. She doesn't say "Called home," which would imply a home in heaven. And she doesn't say "At rest," which would imply the long sleep of the soul. Rather, she is honest enough to sense that her soul is about to complete a cycle of some kind, a return to a source, but whether that source would be the dust or the bosom of God, she doesn't pretend to know. Perhaps in some way it would be both. Her believing, as always, was nimble.

She went into a coma on May 13 and died two days later, probably in the same bed that she envisioned in "I heard a Fly buzz." She was interred in West Cemetery, the burying ground behind the house on West Street where she lived as a girl. Her grave has been the mecca for literary pilgrims for more than a century.[35]

The original marker placed over her grave read simply "E.E.D.," but years later, Martha Dickinson Bianchi, the only daughter of Emily's older brother, Austin, replaced the marker with another, which reads:

EMILY DICKINSON
BORN
DEC. 10, 1830
CALLED BACK
MAY 15, 1886

Things
Guillaume Apollinaire

We quickly get used to the bondage of the mysterious.

"I refute it *thus*!"

With those four words, Samuel Johnson, eighteenth-century England's most renowned man of letters (and William Oldys's friend, as you'll recall), crushed—or at least believed he had crushed—an entire school of philosophy.

The incident was recorded by Johnson's faithful biographer, James Boswell. While the two were passing through Harwich,

England, in 1763, they stopped to tour the crumbling medieval church of St. Nicholas, and they happened to be discussing the philosophy of Bishop George Berkeley at the time. While Berkeley had died a decade earlier, many of his ideas lived on in the writings of such major thinkers as David Hume and Immanuel Kant.

Berkeley's philosophy, called *immaterialism*, was a form of empiricism that proposed that material objects have no independent reality and exist solely in our minds insofar as the senses perceive them. In answer to the age-old question of whether a tree falling in the forest makes a sound if no one is there to hear it, Bishop Berkeley would have said, yes, it does, because God hears it—not because the tree has any sort of physical reality but because all creation exists in the mind of God.

As Boswell and Johnson exited the chapel that day, Boswell commented that while he rejected Berkeley's theory, calling it an "ingenious sophistry to prove the non-existence of matter," he still felt that since everything we know does in fact come to us through our senses, Berkeley's philosophy was difficult to refute.

Without hesitation, Johnson turned to one of the large stones scattered on the ground, kicked it "with mighty force," and declared, "I refute it *thus*!"[1] One can imagine Johnson then stalking off down the lane, no doubt feeling he'd made the world a safer place for common sense and palpability. Had Berkeley been present, he might have responded that since *feeling* is itself one of the senses, all Johnson had proven was that something solid called a stone existed in Johnson's mind.

Of course, Johnson was right in the sense that immaterialism makes no difference to us as we go about our daily lives. We drive to work, eat lunch, and check Instagram—all without the least thought as to whether cars or sandwiches or iPhones exist. Kicking stones still feels like kicking stones whether those stones exist in the mind or elsewhere. Still, Berkeley was surprisingly prescient in ways that even ingenious eighteenth-century clerics couldn't have imagined, for modern quantum theory, astrophysics, and neuroscience have corroborated much of what Berkeley only surmised.

Take, for example, the fact that atoms, which are the building blocks of everything our senses perceive, are for the most part empty space. As Steve Gagnon, a scientist at the US government's Jefferson Lab, points out, a hydrogen atom is 99.9999999999996 percent devoid of any actual physical content. "Put another way," writes Gagnon, "if a hydrogen atom were the size of the earth, the proton at its center would be about 200 meters (600 feet) across."[2] Except for that proton and a single numinous, zero-dimensional electron, the rest of the hydrogen atom is vacant. The rock felt solid to Johnson because of the complex way that electrons interact when atoms come into proximity with each other. These electrons move in preset patterns that only high levels of energy can alter. Johnson's foot lacked sufficient energy to make an appreciable change in the electrons of the rock's atoms so the rock remained immovable—despite the fact that the atoms of the rock as well as of Johnson's shoe were predominantly empty space.

Or consider this: scientists speculate that about 80 percent of the universe is made up of "dark matter"—which is, I imagine, another way of saying "stuff we can't detect with our senses." We assume we can perceive all there is to perceive, but we may have developed only enough awareness of our immediate environment to optimize our chances of survival. We are blind not just to the uncommonly small and the uncommonly large but, more intriguingly, to much of what lies between. Hamlet was right when he said, "There are more things in heaven and earth, Horatio, / Than are dreamt of in your philosophy."[3] In the grand scheme of things, we may only be slightly more aware of the true nature of reality than, say, a soft-shell clam in Chesapeake Bay or, for that matter, a fly on a summer's day.

That, at least, is the theory proposed by some researchers, such as cognitive neuroscientist Donald D. Hoffman at the University of California, Irvine, who comes very close to vindicating Bishop Berkeley. The title of Hoffman's 2019 book sums up his theory: *The Case against Reality: Why Evolution Hid the Truth from Our Eyes*.[4] In a recent article, Hoffman said, "Reality, whatever it is, is too complicated and would take us too much time and energy [to process]. . . . Fitness beats truth. . . . Space is just a data structure, and physical objects are themselves also data structures that we create on the fly."[5]

So what do Berkeley, quantum physics, and neuroscience have to do with French Modernist writer Guillaume Apollinaire, the next poet in this book? The answer, I think, is *everything*. Unlike the other poets we've looked at, Apollinaire doesn't use the fly as a way of talking about something else. It's not a prop. Rather, in his imaginative and curiously roundabout way, he ponders the fly, hoping to find a hint of what its reality might be, to sense its mysterious essence, its thingness. Like so many artists of his time, he was interested not so much in the *why* of things as in the plain, mysteriously elusive *what*.

At the end of the nineteenth century and the beginning of the twentieth, artists were fascinated, to the point of obsession, by our radically changing relationship to the world around us due to technology and science, and they were every bit as intrigued by the psychological and physiological processes we use to perceive that world. Artistic movements like Impressionism, Pointillism, Cubism, Fauvism, Expressionism, and Surrealism rejected the stale, conventional answers to the age-old questions: What is real and how do we know?

Never until our own digital age has the world changed as rapidly or as radically as it did during the short life of Guillaume Apollinaire (1880–1918), which perfectly encompassed what we have since called the dawn of the Modern Age. In his brief thirty-eight years, he saw the advent of the automobile, the airplane, the rocket engine, the dirigible, the motorcycle, and the submarine. Among the technological innovations of that time were the phonograph, the wireless radio, the X-ray machine, mechanized typesetting, offset printing, film animation, and motion pictures (there is even a short silent-film clip from 1914 of Apollinaire chatting with a friend). Between 1900 and 1915, Sigmund Freud published his seminal *Interpretation of Dreams* and *The Psychopathology of Everyday Life*; Marie Curie discovered polonium and radium and coined the term *radioactivity*; Max Planck proposed his Quantum Hypothesis; and Albert Einstein formulated the Theory of Relativity.

If ever a writer lived in the right place at the right time, it was Apollinaire, who, as a poet, novelist, journalist, and critic, became the leading documentarian of artistic Modernism, which arose, in large part, as response to the technological revolution. Although he was born in Italy of Polish-Italian parentage, Apollinaire moved to Paris at age nineteen and soon fell in with a circle of brilliant bohemian artists who were largely unknown at the time, though they would not remain so for long—friends like painters Pablo Picasso, Georges Braque, Marcel Duchamp, Marc Chagall, and Henri Rousseau; writers André Breton, Jean Cocteau, and Gertrude Stein; musician Erik Satie; and many others.

Each in their own way, these artists were on the cutting edge of formulating fresh aesthetic responses to the sometimes exhilarating and sometimes dehumanizing world they found themselves in—a new art for a new age. Picasso, for instance, examined the planar surfaces of his subjects, deconstructing them and painting them from multiple perspectives at once (or as Apollinaire said, "Picasso studies an object as a surgeon dissects a cadaver"[6]). Braque and Duchamp pushed the boundaries of representational art into the realm of abstraction. Cocteau saw potential for film to become as influential an art form as theater and painting. In his score for the avant-garde ballet *Parade*, Erik Satie incorporated such instruments as a typewriter, a police siren, a foghorn, a lottery wheel, and a ticker-tape machine.[7]

In one article after another, Apollinaire chronicled this artistic evolution as it was unfolding and thereby helped to lead the movement as well. He was the first to bring the term *Cubism* into general circulation when he used it to describe an exhibition of paintings in 1911. He later coined the term *Orphism* to describe those artists like Robert Delaunay and František Kupka who moved Cubism in an even less representational and more colorful direction and laid the foundations for modern abstract art.

In 1917, Apollinaire wrote the program notes for the premiere of Erik Satie's *Parade*. If ever there was a confluence of geniuses, it was in the production of that ballet. Cocteau sketched out the enigmatic storyline and Picasso designed the unconventional sets and boxy Cubist-style costumes. The dancers were from Sergei Diaghilev's famous Ballets Russes, which three years earlier had premiered—to furious controversy—Igor Stravinsky's *Rite of Spring*. In his program notes for *Parade*, Apollinaire first proposed the term *Surrealism* to describe the work, and the word stuck—a coinage that came to define an entire movement.

But Apollinaire was at heart a poet, and he was determined that poetry should not be eclipsed by the other arts. In an essay entitled "The New Spirit and the Poets," he wrote:

> It is up to the poets to decide if they will not resolutely embrace the new spirit. . . .
>
> Can poetry . . . ignore the magnificent exuberance of life which the activities of men are adding to nature and which allow the world to be mechanized in an incredible fashion?

The new spirit is the very time in which we are living, a time rich in surprises. The poets wish to master prophecy, that spirited mare that has never been tamed.[8]

The word *prophecy* here is key. For Apollinaire, true poetry is visionary and anticipates the future. Hadn't ancient poets written about Icarus, whose father attached feathers to his arms so he could fly, and then, millennia later, men actually invented airplanes? Hadn't poets, with their vivid imagery and dramatic spectacles, anticipated photography and motion pictures? Modern poets, according to Apollinaire, can't help but extend that ancient tradition; they will "carry you, living and awake, into a nocturnal world sealed with dreams," he wrote, ". . . and more marvels than those which have been born since the birth of the most ancient among us, will make the contemporary inventions of which we are so proud seem pale and childish."[9]

But poetry is prophetic for Apollinaire in another, perhaps more important way. It is visionary—that is, it attempts to see clearly and to delve into the hidden essences of things as they really are. Poetry, he wrote, "*is not a decorative art. Nor is it an impressionist art.* It is every study of exterior and interior nature, it is all eagerness for truth. . . . Even if it is true that there is nothing new under the sun, *the new spirit does not refrain from discovering new profundities in all this that is not new under the sun.*"[10]

Apollinaire first attempted to tame the "spirited mare" of pro-
phetic poetry in 1908, when he published in a literary journal a set
of eighteen poems as a pastiche of the medieval bestiary genre.[11]
Those old bestiaries—"miscellanies of beasts"—were books of
moral instruction and entertainment that described both familiar
and exotic animals and culled devotional lessons from each. For
instance, the pelican symbolizes Christ, for it was believed that a
mother pelican tears open her own breast to feed her chicks with
her blood. The whale is a moral tempter, for its sweet breath was
said to attract small fish into its mouth to be devoured. Though
the science was faulty, the precepts were clear, and the accompany-
ing illustrations were often delightfully fantastic. Those volumes
were among the most popular in the Middle Ages.

When Apollinaire wished to expand his modern bestiary into
a full-length book, he asked Pablo Picasso to provide the illustra-
tions. At first, Picasso warmed to the task, and in the same note-
book that contained his sketches for his groundbreaking Cubist
painting *Les demoiselles d'Avignon*, Picasso sketched some imag-
inary animals intended for the poet's project. But when Apol-
linaire requested that the illustrations be rendered as woodcuts for
printing, Picasso demurred. He had neither time nor patience.

Apollinaire then turned to French Fauvist artist Raoul Dufy,
and an extraordinary partnership was born. They devised a

beautiful *livre d'artiste*, an "artist's book" in which every page displayed an original illustration—printed directly from Dufy's woodcuts—along with one of Apollinaire's short beast poems. Published in 1911, *Le bestiaire, ou cortège d'Orphée* (*The Bestiary, or Procession of Orpheus*) contained thirty conjoined poems and illustrations. Although the volume was a masterpiece, the public response was disappointing. Of the 120 copies printed, only about half sold, though today it's one of the most sought-after books of Modernist literature. In 2011, a copy sold at auction for more than $20,000.

Prophecy in *The Bestiary* is personified by the Greek mythological figure Orpheus, half poet, half seer, who, as the subtitle suggests, is the leader of Apollinaire's "*cortège*," or "procession," of animals. Though he appears in only four of the thirty poems, he is essentially Apollinaire himself, or at least Apollinaire's idealized image of himself, speaking with the poet's own voice—the voice of truth and insight. In the original myth, Orpheus is able to enchant nature itself with his songs, drawing even animals to him. Apollinaire, like Orpheus, gathers the animals together in his short bestiary poems.

Each poem presents an animal in some profound, fanciful, and sometimes mischievous way. The flea, for instance, is compared to a cruel lover who metaphorically sucks the beloved's blood; the mouse symbolizes all those "beautiful days" that secretly nibble away at our lives. The elephant's mouth sprouts ivory, just as the poet wishes for his own mouth to sprout poems, and all "poor poets" can find inspiration in the caterpillar, who will one day turn into a butterfly.[12]

In "La Mouche" ("The Fly"), however, the poet doesn't make a wry joke or a clever observation. Instead, he offers an enigmatic, Orphic answer to this question: Just what *is* a fly?

"The Fly" by Guillaume Apollinaire

> Our flies know songs
> That they learned in Norway
> From ganic flies who are
> The divinities of the snow.[13]

Cryptic. Odd. Baffling, to be sure. But evocative as well.

To explain what flies are, Apollinaire doesn't draw upon science, as Traherne did, or rhetoric or theology. Rather, he turns unexpectedly to the esoteric world of Scandinavian wizardry. Flies, he suggests, don't just buzz; they sing. And they don't sing just any songs; they sing songs they learned from flies in Norway. And not from just any flies, but from flies who are gods to the snowflakes.

And in the midst of that explanation is that impenetrable word *ganic*. It's not found in any French or English dictionary—or Norwegian dictionary, for that matter—and the poet seems to relish it for that very reason. Like the fly itself, it's a cypher. In a note at the end of *The Bestiary* he explains, somewhat unhelpfully, that sorcerers in Lapland keep such flies as deathless, daemonic servants and hand them down from father to son.

His source for this notion was a book published in 1845, *La Finlande*, by a French historian named Louis-Antoine Léouzon Le Duc, who quotes a passage from Italian explorer Giuseppe Acerbi's book, *Travels through Sweden, Finland, and Lapland, and to the North Cape in the Years 1798 and 1799*. Acerbi explains:

> The *ganic flies* are evil spirits entirely under the direction of the Noaaid [sorcerer], and ready at all times to execute his orders; they have been delivered over to him by the Noaaid his father, who received them from his, and so on through a long series of magicians. The ganic flies are invisible to all but the magician, who keeps them shut up in a box until he has occasion for their services.[14]

Knowing that we will be puzzled by his poem and its obscure source, Apollinaire allows us to fill in the blank behind that word *ganic*, a word that strangely means nothing and anything at the same time.

Just as baffling is Dufy's accompanying woodcut, which illustrates something, though most certainly *not* a fly (see figure 9). A true fly has two wings, while Dufy's has four, and its elongated abdomen is much more suggestive of a wasp. The artist was no doubt emulating the fanciful illustrations in the medieval

LA MOUCHE.

Nos mouches savent des chansons
Que leur apprirent en Norvège
Les mouches ganiques qui sont
Les divinités de la neige.

Figure 9. "La Mouche" ("The Fly") from Guillaume Apollinaire's *Le bestiaire, ou cortège d'Orphée* (*The Bestiary, or Procession of Orpheus*), published in 1911 with illustrations by Raoul Dufy.

bestiaries, for elsewhere in the book, his horse and ox both have wings and his caterpillar is actually a centipede. Dufy was aiming not at accurate portrayal but at something deeper and more intuitive. This, he seems to be saying, is what a fly looks like to his mind's eye. "Instead of painting objects as they saw them," wrote art critic Maurice Raynal, a friend of Apollinaire's, the new artists "painted them as they thought them."[15]

So, does Apollinaire believe that Finnish sorcery is the true essence of fly-ness, that flies are really invisible, immortal gods that are worshipped by the snow?

Probably not, but that's the wrong question. Apollinaire's poem is no more literal or representational than Dufy's illustration. It is, rather, visionary, and to that extent it seeks a different truth, a hidden and prophetic truth. As Picasso once said, "We all know that Art is not truth. Art is a lie that makes us realize truth, at least the truth that is given us to understand."[16] Apollinaire is not teaching a lesson or searching for moral precepts. He is opening himself to the possibility of perceiving, as he said, "*new profundities to all this that is not new under the sun.*"

In the new era of technological upheaval, things were no longer just things. They were intimations, "shadows," as Blake wrote, of "the real & eternal World" of the imagination.[17] As science was discovering, the essence of the physical world was far different than humans had imagined for millennia. Apollinaire writes, "Science undoes and remakes what already exists, whole worlds disappear forever from our understanding. . . . We quickly get used to the bondage of the mysterious."[18] An incomprehensible whirling power dwells inside the atoms that make up everything in the world, space and time are no longer stable but warped and variable, radio messages can zoom invisibly through the air, and X-rays can peer inside objects and even through them. Not only are objects numinous and mysterious, but our ability to perceive them is unreliable—like peering through a mist with steam-fogged glasses.

In "The Fly," Apollinaire's goal was to reawaken the senses, to suggest new possibilities for the new era that had shaken up old certainties and overturned conventional understandings. We shouldn't take the lowly fly—or anything in this world—for granted, because when viewed from different angles, the way the Cubists viewed their subjects, everything is odd and perplexing. In his imaginative way, Apollinaire was encouraging us to be fascinated by the inscrutable thingness of things. You may think you know what a fly is, Apollinaire is saying, but you don't. As Orpheus says in one of the *Bestiary* poems, mites, insects, and microbes, "the thousand-footed and hundred-eyed," are "more marvelous / than the seven wonders of the world."[19]

Nor is language itself any less inscrutable. In this new age of unreliable and shifting appearances, words shed their meanings and cease to evoke the objects they represent, which is why Apollinaire gives us that word *ganic*; it encompasses much while remaining indefinable. American writer Gertrude Stein, a friend of Apollinaire's, once defended her much-parodied line "Rose is a rose is a rose is a rose" this way:[20]

> Can't you see that when the language was new, as it was with Chaucer and Homer—the poet could use the name of the thing and the thing was really there. . . . And can't you see that after hundreds of years had gone by and thousands of poems had been written, he could call on those words and find that they were just worn-out literary words. . . . We all know that it's hard to write poetry in a late age; and we know that you have to put some strangeness, something unexpected, into the sentence in order to bring vitality back to the noun.[21]

Bringing "strangeness" and "vitality" back to the commonplace things all around us—be they objects, colors, shapes, words, sensations—is as good a definition of Modernism as I can think of.

✦ ✦ ✦

So why should we care about strangeness and vitality?

Because they were our original state. Such was the world into which we were born, a world infused with a mystifying Light and Presence. Everything we experienced as infants was strange and alive—and not just in a figurative sense but with a vitality, a *livingness*, that flowed all around us and through us and in us. If only we could remember, renew our experience of that time. In the prologue of this book, we looked at a number of poets who in their own Orpheus-like way tried to define that state of wonder, though they used other words to describe it. William Wordsworth called it "the glory and freshness of a dream,"[22] Henry Vaughan called it "Bright shoots of everlastingness,"[23] C. S. Lewis called it "Joy . . . the moments of clearest consciousness we had,"[24] and Thomas Traherne, quite succinctly, called it Felicity.

Twentieth-century British philosopher Owen Barfield used another word for that state: *participation*. That was the time when our perceptions were not objective, set in isolation, but were a part of everything we experienced. We had not yet learned to think directly about the world (what Barfield calls "alpha-thinking") or about the fact that we even had thoughts (what he calls "beta-thinking"). Those states of consciousness would come later, through maturity and education. But in infancy we perceived the world differently, newly, as if from *inside*. We were part of it, breathed it in and were breathed in by it, interwoven into its odd miraculousness simply by being there.

Later, once we've learned to reflect on the things we perceive, and to reflect on our reflecting, we end up objectifying both the world and our experience of it. We see ourselves as separate, as observers rather than participants. That original Light fades, and the result, theologically, is that we objectify our experiences of the Divine as well, making God an object of study, a focus of worship, a target for prayer—while losing a sense of God as Presence and Sustainer, the vast Everything of which we are a part.

In one of his books, significantly called *Saving the Appearances*, Barfield rejects Berkeley's immaterialism as irrelevant to our daily lives, and he rejects Johnson's cantankerous stone-kicking as well. Both Berkeley and Johnson assume that only alpha- and beta-thinking are real, that knowledge comes through the senses—empirically. Those philosophers failed to see another, deeper way of being—in the primal experiences of precognitive participation. In the words of science writer Tim Folger, "Reality is not completely objective—we cannot separate ourselves from the world we observe."[25] The following lines from a poem by my wife, Shelley Townsend-Hudson, get at that same alternate way of being:

> At first, things existed by imprint, then named
> and treasured until everything came together
> without the slightest seam. But before then,
> trees, when first seen, unlabeled, were strange,
> so very, very strange.[26]

Barfield sees this process taking place in the evolution of human consciousness itself, throughout humankind's history. Not unlike infants, our earliest ancestors—like primitive societies still—experienced an unadulterated participation in the world, but as societies grew more civilized through time, humans lost that sense of harmony. They lost Felicity.

The fact is that we can never return to that original state of consciousness. But we can, according to Barfield, catch glimpses of it. For brief moments we are able recapture those "Bright shoots of everlastingness" through aesthetic experiences, by opening ourselves to the intimations of Beauty—especially through poetry. (C. S. Lewis's concept of Joy, which he outlines in his book *Surprised by Joy*, grew out of his conversations with Barfield, who was a close friend.) For Apollinaire, Orpheus was the ideal poet of that original state, for his voice—and the voice of all true poets, according to Apollinaire in one of the *Bestiary* poems—was "the voice that Light itself caused to be heard."[27] Poetry give us flashes of illumination.

The key ingredient of that illumination is exactly the kind of strangeness that Gertrude Stein talked about. Barfield wrote, "That 'element of strangeness in all beauty,' . . . has been remarked in one way or another by so many critics. Alike in the greatest poetry and in the least, if pleasure is to arise, it must be there."[28]

✦ ✦ ✦

This explains why so many Modernists embraced primitivism. In ancient civilizations and in aboriginal cultures, Modernist artists found a reconnection to an authentic, visceral, pre-alpha-thinking reality. They were awakened to a kind of alien poeticism. In an essay on Cubism, Apollinaire called on artists to abandon conventional ways of looking at the world and to move into "the fourth dimension," which, he said, "has come to stand for the aspirations and premonitions of many young artists who contemplate Egyptian, negro, and oceanic sculpture, meditate on various scientific works, and live in anticipation of a sublime art."[29] Picasso collected African masks and incorporated them into such paintings as *Les demoiselles d'Avignon*; Henri Rousseau painted jungle scenes with African animals and figures; Stravinsky's ballet *The Rite of Spring* portrayed an ancient, pagan sacrificial rite.

So, in answer to the question *What is a fly?*, Apollinaire, by looking to the primitivism of both Greek myth and Finnish sorcery, is answering, in a sense, that *he* is the fly. He participates in its primal essence just as he participates in the essence of all the animals in his *Bestiary*. The fly that sings those ancient, mystical songs, which they learned from immortal Finnish *ganic* flies—*that* fly is Apollinaire, reaching back through the millennia in his visionary way, channeling the prophetic voice of Orpheus "in anticipation of a sublime art." Orpheus, who is both the poet and fly at once, doesn't listen to the "dangerous and inhuman" sirens, according to one of Apollinaire's bestiary poems, but only to "the Angels of heaven."[30]

Apollinaire's passion for prophecy and poetry were symptomatic of his longing for the ancient and universal, the authentic and transcendent, the visceral and primal. In his notes at the end of *The Bestiary*—the book's final sentence, in fact—the poet made this declaration: "Those who practice poetry seek and love nothing other than perfection, which is God himself."[31] Apollinaire longed to see beyond the surfaces of the things in this "Vegetable Universe," as Blake called it—to see them as they are. To both Bishop Berkeley and Dr. Johnson, Apollinaire would have said, the things of this world are not just things; they are mysteries that dwell in the deepest parts of ourselves.

7

Story
Robert Farren

a fleeting glimpse of Joy, Joy beyond the walls of the world

So, who *is* your favorite poet?

If you're like me, you draw a blank when you're asked that question. There are, of course, all those old classic poets you return to again and again, like literary comfort food—poets that you picture yourself reading by the fire on long winter nights. Or if you read much poetry, then you also try to keep up with all these new, young poets whose freshness and unexpectedness take your breath away—poets whose books you slip from the local bookstore's shelves and read in the store's café. In other words, too many poets to choose from.

Curiously, though, when someone asks for a favorite poem, I don't hesitate. I say "The Pets" by twentieth-century Irish poet Robert Farren, which is especially curious to me because I know it's *not* a great poem. It's not one of those immortal verses that's likely to captivate readers centuries from now, nor is it, as we'll see, entirely original. And I'd never think to include Farren on my list of classic, comfort-food poets.

But I've loved "The Pets" ever since I first discovered it in *The Oxford Book of Irish Verse* decades ago,[1] and the fact that I love it makes me realize that a poem doesn't have to be great and immortal to be someone's favorite. It simply needs to fill an empty space in one's soul that no other poem can fill. The corollary for poets is this: Don't strive to be great; strive to be human. For all of us poets who will probably never write an immortal poem, it's a comfort to know that we might still write a poem that can fill such a place in some anonymous someone's life.

So, this simple, plain-spoken, whimsical poem by an obscure twentieth-century Irish poet fills that place for me.

✦ ✦ ✦

"The Pets" (from *The First Exile*) by Robert Farren

Colm had a cat,
and a wren,
and a fly.

The cat was a pet,
and the wren,
and the fly.

And it happened that the wren
ate the fly;
and it happened that the cat
ate the wren.

Then the cat died.

So Saint Colm lacked a cat,
and a wren,
and a fly.

But Saint Colm loved the cat,
and the wren,
and the fly,

so he prayed to get them back,
cat and wren;
and he prayed to get them back,
wren and fly.

And the cat became alive
and delivered up the wren;
and the wren became alive
and delivered up the fly;
and they all lived with Colm
till the day came to die.

First the cat died.
Then the wren died.
Then the fly.[2]

✦ ✦ ✦

Poet and playwright Robert Farren, whose Irish name was Roibeard Ó Faracháin, was born in Dublin in 1909, the son of a stone mason. At that time, Ireland was at the height of its great literary renaissance, led by such monumental figures as William Butler Yeats, Lady Gregory, and John Millington Synge. It was a time that saw an unprecedented burst of literary creativity, fueled by an insurgent nationalism and a passion for preserving Ireland's Celtic roots. Yeats referred to the era as the Celtic Revival. It was also the time when Ireland was in the fraught and violent process of wresting its independence from England, and it was into this heady world of rejuvenation and turmoil that Robert Farren was born.

Farren was educated in the Catholic schools of Dublin and eventually received a teaching degree from St. Patrick's Training College. After earning a master's degree in Thomistic philosophy from University College Cork, he got a job teaching at a boys' school, where he managed to find time to pursue his true passion—poetry—and to publish two volumes of verse. But teaching, he discovered, was not to his taste. He later wrote a humorous poem, called "School Teacher," in which he described the "torture" and "bone-grinding agony" of a teacher's life; it was, he wrote, like trying "to bore through thick-ribbed concrete of stupidity."[3] So, at the age of thirty, just as Europe was sliding into the maelstrom of the Second World War, he began a new career—as a program director at Raidió Teilifís Éireann—RTÉ—Ireland's (and, in fact, the world's) first public radio station.

Among his friends at RTÉ was poet and journalist Austin Clarke, a leading figure in the Irish Renaissance of the generation after Yeats. As a result of Farren and Clarke's shared interest in spoken poetry and in reviving ancient Gaelic prosody, they founded an experimental theater, one that would primarily feature plays written in verse. Called the Irish Lyric Theatre, it opened in 1944 in a large downstairs room in Dublin's famed Abbey Theatre, which Yeats himself had established four decades earlier. Farren worked with the Lyric and Abbey Theatres as well as RTÉ for the next three decades, and he was instrumental in adapting many stage plays for the radio.

The writers of the Irish Literary Revival, who found inspiration in the country's traditional folklore and fairytales, tended to view Christianity's eclipse of the ancient Celtic gods—which Yeats called the Celtic Twilight—as something that was both tragic and inevitable. As a result, they sometimes neglected, even denigrated, the island's early Catholic saints—an oversight that Farren was determined to remedy. He believed that those doughty, bigger-than-life saints were every bit as heroic as such mythic figures as Oisin, Finn Mac Cool, and Cuchulain.

So during the early part of the war, Farren composed an epic narrative poem—actually a series of seventy-seven interconnected poems—on the life of Colm, the influential sixth-century monk and abbot. The work was titled *The First Exile*, and one of the poems in that collection was "The Pets."[4] Farren could not have chosen a more enthralling figure for his epic, because Colm was not only the stuff of legend, he had the advantage of having one foot firmly planted in historical records. As a bonus, Colm was a poet.

Colm—also called Columba ("the dove") or Colmcille ("the church dove")—was the third and last of the three great patron saints of Ireland, after Saint Brigid of Kildare and, of course, Saint Patrick (see figure 10). A vast number of fantastic tales accrued to Saint Colm over the centuries. For instance, in Scotland he is said to have driven off a deadly water monster that was attacking villagers along the River Ness—which some authorities suggest is history's first reference to the Loch Ness monster.

Colm was unusually gifted at casting out demons. He once exorcised a bucket of milk in which an evil spirit had taken up residence, though the bucket tipped over in the process. Still, Colm, not one to cry over spilt milk, managed to not only dispel the demon but restore the bucket's contents as well. Another

Figure 10. Saints Colm, Patrick, and Brigid, the three patron saints of Ireland. An illustration from the title page of *Florilrgium insulae sanctorum* ("Selections from the Island of the Saints") by Thomas Messingham, Paris, 1624. It is tempting to think that the creature at Colm's feet is the cat referred to in "The Pets," but it is most likely one of the many demons that Colm is said to have cast out.

time, he transformed a host of demons into fish and cast them into the sea. Thereafter, according to legend, whenever a fisherman found an unfamiliar fish in his net, he would toss it back and say a quick prayer to Saint Colm.

The saint had a special relationship with animals, or as Farren phrased it, "O Father Colm was gentle / to creeping and cantering kind."[5] He once nursed a weather-beaten crane back to health, a bird whose arrival from across the sea Colm had even prophesied. Another time, after he blessed a poor farmer's five haggard cows, the herd quickly grew to more than a hundred. When some sailors told Colm of a certain whale that terrified them, Colm conferred a special blessing upon the sea and reassured them, "That monster and I are under the power of God."[6]

But Colm was far from being an Irish Saint Francis. In fact, he's thought to have been the spark that ignited a war. It happened like this: as a monk in his late thirties, Colm asked a certain abbot named Finnian (later Saint Finnian), for permission to copy a rare Latin psalter from the abbey's scriptorium. Working at night, by a mysterious light provided by Providence, Colm produced his copy. When it was complete, he assumed he'd be allowed to keep it, but the abbot thought otherwise, insisting that the copy belonged to him. After a furious argument, the matter was referred to Diarmait Mac Cerbhaill, who was then high king of Ireland, and Diarmait ruled in favor of Abbot

Finnian, proclaiming, "To every cow belongs her calf, therefore to every book belongs its copy."[7]

Unhappy with the verdict, Colm appealed to members of the two clans to which he was related, and they in turn used his grievance as an excuse to mount a rebellion against the king. The climactic battle took place around 561 in what is now County Sligo, a battle in which thousands were said to have been killed, and ever since, it has been referred to as the Battle of the Book, or (in Gaelic) Cúl Dreimhne. In his narrative, Farren summarizes its outcome this way:

> Colm gained the book,
> encased it in leather,
> silver and gold;
> then he blessed it
> then he named it
> *An Cathach, The Battler.*[8]

Today, the Irish Royal Academy Library has in its archives fifty-eight vellum pages from what are believed to be Colm's own hand-lettered copy of that psalter. The manuscript is indeed called the Cathach, the "Battle Book."[9]

But for Colm, the battle was hardly a victory. He soon regretted his actions and grieved for the lives that were lost. As an act of penance, he exiled himself from Ireland so he might dedicate the rest of his life to evangelizing the unruly Picts along the coasts of Scotland and northern England—a difficult mission at best. His desperate goal was to convert at least as many souls as had been lost in the war. As an additional penance, he would walk daily along the shore and recite, or rather shout, the Psalms, which he had memorized, into the blasting wind and spray of the Scottish sea. While Colm's faith was great, he had no illusions about the difficulty of his mission. He wrote:

> [I am] a little man,
> shivering and miserable,
> rowing through the infinite tempest
> of this age.[10]

But the work proved successful. In 563, he undertook the ambitious project that is now most associated with his name: the founding of an abbey on the barren, wind-swept island of Iona off the western coast of Scotland. Using the island as a base of operations, he and the twelve monks who followed him managed to convert much of Scotland and parts of England to Christianity, including, according to some records, the Pictish king Bridei. In the centuries that followed, Iona became one of the most influential monastic centers in Europe, preserving literacy and culture during the so-called Dark Ages, and sending missionaries throughout the known world. The familiar image of the Celtic cross (see figure 11) first appeared on the island in its many stone monuments, and it is most likely where the famed Book of Kells was produced.

✦ ✦ ✦

Robert Farren's primary source for *The First Exile* was a biography of Colm written by a monk named Adamnan, who lived on Iona

Figure 11. A Celtic cross. This is Saint Martin's High Cross, one of the oldest crosses on Iona, dating from the latter half of the eighth century, two centuries after the time of Saint Colm. Few remnants from Saint Colm's era remain.[11]

a hundred years after the renowned saint. Adamnan's book was a catalog of dozens of anecdotes about the prophecies, miracles, and visions of Iona's great saint, including the accounts of the monster in the River Ness and the overturned bucket of milk.

Farren also consulted a later and lesser-known volume, which was first translated from Gaelic into English just twenty years before Farren began researching his epic. That biography, *Betha Colaim Chille: The Life of Columcille*, was compiled from a variety of sources by a sixteenth-century Irish prince named Manus O'Donnell, and it included a number of stories not found in Adamnan—in particular, the curious anecdote about the pets. Here is O'Donnell's version:

> There were three pets that Columcille had, a cat and a wren and a fly. . . . And it happened that the wren ate the fly and the cat ate the wren. . . . And such love had Columcille for those little creatures of his, that he asked God to revive them for him, to get back the fly from the wren, and the wren from the cat. And he obtained that from God. And they were with him thenceforth as they were before, till they had lived out their lives according to nature. Wherefore he made this quatrain:
>
>> The deed they have done.
>> If God wills it, may He hear me:

> May He get from my cat my wren:
> May He get from my wren my fly.[12]

Farren followed the translation closely, even borrowing word-for-word such phrases as "a cat and a wren and a fly" and "it happened that the wren ate the fly." But he does a number of things to stamp the poem as his own. First, by dispensing with such stuffy words as "thenceforth" and "wherefore," he simplifies the language, so that "The Pets" becomes a poem made up almost entirely of one-syllable words. Of the poem's one hundred and thirty words, all but eight are monosyllables, which gives the poem the lilt of a children's nursery rhyme. At the same time, he streamlines the narrative to its essentials—a clear beginning, middle, and end—to give it the spare efficiency of an Aesop's fable.

Rhythmically, Farren's verse is brilliant, with much of its power coming from his meticulous avoidance of traditional iambic rhythm. Like so many of the roughhewn ancient Irish poems Farren loved, "The Pets" is full of multiple unaccented syllables preceded or followed by a strongly accented syllable (variations of dactyls and anapests); for instance, "Then it *hap*pened that the *wren* / ate the *fly*"; and then two strong syllables (spondees) are occasionally thrown in for special emphasis, as in, "Then the *cat died.*" A primitive kind of ruggedness is achieved, wholly appropriate for a sixth-century saint who, as we noted, would recite psalms into the cold blasts of the ocean's winds.

Farren's use of repetition gives the poem an incantatory drive—that is, the poem resembles a spoken charm, a magic spell over Nature itself. Of those hundred and thirty words, only forty different words are used. The rest are repeated, and two-thirds of the poem's thirty lines end with the words *cat* or *wren* or *fly*. Such repetition is a deliberate echo of the old Celtic chants and prayers that inspired so many of the writers of the Celtic Revival, as in this ancient Scottish invocation:

> The best hour of the day be thine,
> The best day of the week be thine,
> The best week of the year be thine,
> The best year in the Son of God's domain be thine.[13]

But "The Pets" is more than a nursery rhyme or an incantation; it's a story, worthy to stand alongside any of the folktales of the Celtic Revival. Within its bare-boned narrative, Farren manages to evoke a world that is as fantastic as anything in the novels of J. R. R. Tolkien or C. S. Lewis—a magical place where a fly can be a pet, where belief is as natural as breathing, where prayers are heard and answered, a world of tragedy and mischance as well as miracle and inexplicable mystery.

Farren's addition of the imaginative plot twist at the end (a detail not found in O'Donnell's original account) makes the poem entirely the poet's own. Although the average fly lives between twenty and thirty days, Colm's fly, after its resuscitation, outlives both the cat and the wren: "First the cat died. / Then the wren died. / Then the fly."

This wonderful reversal is why I love "The Pets," why it fills me with not only joy but immense hope. When the poet says that the pets "lived with Colm / till the day came to die," he implies not just the pets' deaths but Colm's as well, and his own resurrection in heaven, a new life that was foreshadowed by the fly's emergence from the double tomb of the wren and the cat. "The last enemy that shall be destroyed," says the apostle Paul, "is death."[14]

In his essay "On Fairy-Stories," Tolkien, that master inventor of tales, once coined a word to describe this kind of reversal, when victory emerges from the ashes of defeat. He called it *eucatastrophe* (the word *catastrophe* prefixed with the Greek *eu*, meaning "happy"—a happy catastrophe). It is the moment when seemingly imminent disaster is averted and joy is restored. It's a hallmark of fairy stories worldwide—whenever a prince arrives to save the day or an evil spell is lifted or a fairy godmother intervenes. In Tolkien's own tale *The Hobbit*, the eagles and Beron, in the nick of time, arrive to defeat the goblins and wolves at the Battle of the Five Armies. In his Lord of the Rings trilogy, Gandalf is nearly a one-man dispenser of eucatastrophe.

Such stories, writes Tolkien, exhibit "a sudden and miraculous grace: never to be counted on to recur." Eucatastrophe is neither comic nor tragic—as represented by those two classic Greek masks often found in theaters, one grinning broadly, the other howling in grief. Rather, Tolkien continues:

> It does not deny the existence of *dyscatastrophe*, of sorrow and failure: the possibility of these is necessary to the joy of deliverance; it denies (in the face of much evidence, if you will) universal final defeat . . . , giving a fleeting glimpse of Joy, Joy beyond the walls of the world, poignant as grief.[15]

Despite the fairytale elements of Farren's story, Saint Colm himself originally told the tale of the pets, according to Manus O'Donnell, with a serious political and even prophetic intent. Like the wren eating the fly, some of the Irish, or the "Gaels" as they were known, were persecuting Christians and shutting down their churches, and for this sin, Colm warned, the Gaels ran the risk of someday being devoured themselves by foreign invaders, symbolized by the cat. "Thus men should do in a later time," said Colm in O'Donnell's account, "the strong of them should eat the weak," and as long as Ireland remained disobedient to God, "the power of foreigners should be over them." This prophecy came true in a startling way two centuries later when the Vikings invaded the island.

But Colm understood that this coming invasion might well be a blessing in disguise—a eucatastrophe. Colm prophesied that, just as the cat "rendered up the wren," the Irish would one day regain their independence, or, as Colm said, "Whenever right and justice were kept, . . . then shall God give back again to the Gaels their strength and might,"[16] a prophecy that has as much relevance to the last century of Irish history—to the Irish War of Independence—as it does to the age of the Vikings.

Then, like the wren rendering up the fly, the church itself would be restored. So the fact that the fly, which symbolizes the church's weak and oppressed community, outlives both the cat and wren is not nearly as fantastic as it sounds. Colm is saying, in effect, that the kingdom of God will outlive the kingdoms of the world. "Blessed are the meek," said Jesus, "for they shall inherit the earth."[17]

So Saint Colm's Iona is not just a fairytale world. It is our own world seen from the outside, from the perspective of history, of eternity. It is, like Tolkien's Middle Earth or Lewis's Narnia, so much like the world we inhabit that when we hear it described in terms of a Divine eucatastrophe we hardly recognize it at all.

While "The Pets" is about Ireland in the sixth century, it is about us as well, about our own country in our own time.

Colm's story of the cat and wren and fly still speaks to us fifteen centuries later. Its prophetic message is this: Who are the weak and oppressed that our own country is devouring? And who, like the cat, will devour us if we fail to restore "right and justice"? However we answer those questions, Colm also assures us that the remnant—the tiny, weak, humble fly of the community of the faithful—will outlive all the nations on earth.

The point of these tales about Colm—and the point of all the saints' lives, for that matter—is to teach lessons about who we are, how we should live, and what the nature of the Holy is. Such stories give us joy and hope; they warn us and convict us as well. Stories, you see, are conveyors of *grace*, which can be defined as all those unmerited gifts, whether physical or spiritual, that Providence bestows upon humans. As English Metaphysical poet George Herbert wrote, "Thy graces without cease / Drop from above!"[18]

In the traditional Christian view, the function of the sacraments, like Communion, baptism, marriage, and so on, is to transmit grace from God to the believer. But that leads me to this important question: Why isn't story itself one of the sacraments? So much of the grace we experience day to day—nearly everything we know, learn, believe, and hold dear—comes to us wrapped in stories. Without them, we can't begin to make sense of our sometimes meandering and often mysterious passage through life. Colm made sense of his time by telling his parable about the pets, and Robert Farren, in taking up Colm's story, made sense of his time by writing *The First Exile*.

Think about how stories help explain you to yourself: the story of how you came into the world, your earliest memory, your childhood friends, how you met your partner, how you managed to survive a serious illness or avoid a near-fatal accident, how you came to faith. As the psalmist wrote, "We spend our years as a tale that is told."[19] And each of those stories convey a message of grace.

Of all the sacraments that theologians tell us are conduits of grace, Jesus rarely, and in some cases never, administered them himself. But what Jesus *did* do was tell stories. Lots of stories. A wayward son is welcomed home by his loving father. Laborers are paid a full day's wage even though they arrived late in the day. A man buys a field with buried treasure. A shepherd keeps searching until a lost sheep is found.

The resurrection itself would be a meaningless doctrine, almost nonsensical, without the story that goes with it. "The Birth of Christ," wrote Tolkien, "is the eucatastrophe of Man's history. The Resurrection is the eucatastrophe of the story of the Incarnation. This story begins and ends in joy."[20]

Grace, in other words, is in the telling.

Christians commonly refer to their message as the good news, but I wonder if a more appropriate translation might be the good story. Every time we hear a tale—or tell one—about hope and restoration, whether it's "The Pets" or the Gospel of John, I suspect that Jesus dwells somewhere deep inside it. Imagine the joy that Mary Magdalene must have felt when, after seeing the resurrected Christ at the tomb, she ran back to Jerusalem "and told the disciples" the story of the eucatastrophe that had just taken place.[21] It was a story so full of grace that it changed history. "Whenever you tell a good story," Jesus might have said to his disciples, "do it in remembrance of me."

And whether that good story begins with "Once upon a time" or "Colm had a cat, / and a wren, / and a fly" or "In the beginning was the Word, and the Word was with God," we should never doubt that it takes place in a strange and miraculous country, which is in fact our own.

Epilogue
Mystery and Faith

A fly went by.

When I was first learning to read in the late 1950s, my favorite book (believe it or not) was Mike McClintock's *A Fly Went By*, illustrated by Fritz Siebel (see figure 12).[1] In it, a boy sees a fly zip past. When he asks the fly why it's in such a hurry, the fly explains that a frog is chasing it. When the boy asks the frog why it's chasing the fly, the frog explains that it wasn't chasing the fly at all but fleeing from the cat. The cat, in turn, was running from

Figure 12. Frontispiece illustration by Fritz Siebel for Mike McClintock's *A Fly Went By* (1958). Used by permission.

the dog, and on and on until the boy finally discovers the source of the final animal's panic: a baby goat was making a racket because the handle of a bucket had gotten looped over its back leg and he couldn't shake it off. Mystery solved.

Each of the poets in *The Poet and the Fly*—from Thomas Traherne to Robert Farren—saw a fly zip past and was confronted by a mystery:

- Thomas Traherne encountered Felicity—the inexplicable notion that the entire universe had been made expressly for him alone—and for you alone as well.

- William Oldys grappled with the paradox that the shortness of life adds richness to life.
- William Blake found the vast, holy Creator of the universe had taken up residence in his own imagination.
- Kobayashi Issa, through a prayer for a solitary fly, thereby expressed compassion for every suffering soul on earth.
- Emily Dickinson discovered that faith—which is sometimes another word for doubt—can embrace unimaginable contradictions.
- Guillaume Apollinaire perceived that ordinary things are far stranger and more vibrant than we ever imagined.
- And Robert Farren found grace in the simple telling of a story about a saint.

The point of this book was not to solve these mysteries, to answer the hard questions and dispel the niggling doubts. In fact, the point was just the opposite—to heighten the mystery that each poet faced. The truth is that some mysteries are not meant to be solved. They exist for their sheer beauty alone, much like those intricate, labyrinthine knots that you find in Celtic art, which are not meant to be unraveled but to be marveled at.

In a sense, this book, then, has been my own statement of faith. After years of being told and taught and preached at about what I'm supposed to believe and not believe, I've come to the simple conclusion that there are a lot of things I can't figure out and perhaps am not meant to. I've grown as comfortable with the unknown and unknowable as with the known and knowable, because for me, faith is not about having the answers but about finding a home in my life for mystery, for doubt, for the tantalizing "what ifs" of existence, and for trusting that the next footstep I take, however tentative it is and wherever it leads, is exactly the one I was meant to take. Faith is reveling in the wonders around us rather than having to explain and objectify them, for Whoever Is Out There, Whatever Is Transcendent is speaking through them every bit as much as through the dust motes drifting through the sun shafts I saw as a baby.

Of course, there are countless other mysteries that this book hasn't even hinted at: memory, prayer, sorrow, longing, self-sacrifice, gratitude, music, touch, light, language, joy, and love, to mention only a few. How fascinating it would be to read what the great writers have to say on those subjects. Imagine if we could read what poets, past and present, have to say about all those other things that are so common, like the fly, that we take them for granted: clouds or trees, hands or faces, the color blue or frost in winter, flowers or waterfalls, toadstools or toads. Poets have written about all those things. Imagine what we could learn from a book entitled *The Poet and the Mouse* or even one called *The Poet and the Elephant*! The list is as large as the world itself, because our world is a realm of limitless wonder, or perhaps more like a vast and beautiful Celtic knot.

But those books will have to be left for another time and for other writers because this one has now reached its end, and I can think of no more perfect way to conclude than to quote the Roman satirist Lucian, who ended his essay "In Praise of the Fly" with this disclaimer:

> Though I still have a great deal more to say,
> I will stop talking,
> for fear you may think that,
> as the saying goes,
> I am making an elephant out of a fly.[2]

Appendix
A Few More Fly Poems

Poets have been fascinated by flies for millennia. The Greek poet Homer once compared a great warrior not to a lion or an eagle but to a fly, because the fly was capable of "unshrinking and persistent assault . . . not mere audacity, but courage."[1] Some ancient scholars report that the Roman poet Virgil held an elaborate funeral for a dead fly and buried it in a specially prepared tomb, though if true, it was probably done as a ruse to keep the Roman authorities from confiscating his property; burial sites were considered sacred and therefore off limits to the government.

So, as you read these additional fly poems, which date from the sixth century BCE to the present, ask yourself, "What fascinated this poet about the fly? And what mystery is the poet exploring?"

"Dirge" by Simonides of Ceos (ca. 556–468 BCE)

Human, never presume to know what tomorrow will
    bring
or, when you see someone happy, how long they'll stay
    that way.
Not even the long-winged fly
changes its place so quickly.[2]

From *Titus Andronicus* by William Shakespeare (1564–1616)

(MARCUS strikes the dish with a knife)

TITUS ANDRONICUS. What dost thou strike at, Marcus,
    with thy knife?

MARCUS ANDRONICUS. At that that I have kill'd, my lord;
    a fly.

TITUS ANDRONICUS. Out on thee, murderer! thou kill'st
    my heart;

Mine eyes are cloy'd with view of tyranny:
A deed of death done on the innocent
Becomes not Titus' brother: get thee gone:
I see thou art not for my company.

MARCUS ANDRONICUS. Alas, my lord, I have but kill'd
a fly.
TITUS ANDRONICUS. But how, if that fly had a father and
mother?
How would he hang his slender gilded wings,
And buzz lamenting doings in the air!
Poor harmless fly,
That, with his pretty buzzing melody,
Came here to make us merry! and thou hast kill'd
him.[3]

"The Amber Bead" by Robert Herrick (1591–1674)

I saw a fly within a bead
Of amber cleanly buried;
The urn was little, but the room
More rich than Cleopatra's tomb.[4]

"Complaining" by George Herbert (1593–1633)

Do not beguile my heart,
Because thou art
My power and wisdom. Put me not to shame,
Because I am
Thy clay that weeps, thy dust that calls.

Thou art the Lord of glory;
The deed and story
Are both thy due: but I a silly fly,
That live or die
According as the weather falls.

Art thou all justice, Lord?
Shows not thy work
More attributes? Am I all throat or eye,
To weep or cry?
Have I no parts but those of grief?

Let not thy wrathful power
Afflict my hour,
My inch of life: or let thy gracious power
Contract my hour,
That I may climb and find relief.[5]

"The Coach and the Fly" by Jean de La Fontaine (1621–1695)

Upon a sandy uphill road,
Which naked in the sunshine glowed,
Six lusty horses drew a coach.
Dames, monks, and invalids, its load,
On foot, outside, at leisure trode.
The team, all weary, stepped and blowed:
Whereon there did a fly approach,

And with a vastly business air,
 Cheered up the horses with his buzz—
Now pricked them here, now pricked them there,
 As neatly as a jockey does—
And thought the while—he knew 'twas so—
He made the team and carriage go—
On carriage pole sometimes alighting—
Or driver's nose—and biting.
And when the whole did get in motion,
Confirmed and settled in the notion,
He took himself, the total glory—
Flew back and forth in wondrous hurry,
And as he flew about the cattle,
Seemed like a sergeant in a battle,
The flies and squadrons leading on
To where the victory is won.
Thus charged with all the commonweal
This single fly began to feel
Responsibility too great,
And cares, a grievous crushing weight;
And made complaint that none would aid
 The horses up the tedious hill—
The monk his prayers at leisure said—
 Fine time to pray!—the dames, at will,
Were singing songs—not greatly needed!
 Thus in their ears he sharply sang,
 And notes of indignation ran—
Notes, after all, not greatly heeded.

Erelong the coach was on the top:
"Now," said the fly, "my hearties, stop
And breathe—I've got you up the hill;
 And Messrs. Horses, let me say,
I need not ask you if you will
 A proper compensation pay."

Thus certain ever-bustling noddies
 Are seen in every great affair;
Important, swelling, busybodies
 And bores 'tis easier to bear
Than chase them from their needless care.[6]

Haiku by Matsuo Bashō (1644–1694)

follow the way
of the resolute pilgrim—
flies of Kiso[7]

Haiku by Hattori Ransetsu (1654–1707)

I dare you, fly,
to steal the rice grain
from my chin[8]

From "Ode on the Spring" by Thomas Gray (1716–1771)

To Contemplation's sober eye
Such is the race of man:
And they that creep, and they that fly,
Shall end where they began.
Alike the busy and the gay
But flutter through life's little day,
In fortune's varying colours dressed:
Brushed by the hand of rough Mischance,
Or chilled by age, their airy dance
They leave, in dust to rest.

Methinks I hear in accents low
The sportive kind reply:
"Poor moralist! and what art thou?
A solitary fly!
Thy joys no glittering female meets,
No hive hast thou of hoarded sweets,
No painted plumage to display:
On hasty wings thy youth is flown;
Thy sun is set, thy spring is gone—
We frolic, while 'tis May."[9]

"Law" by James Beattie (1735–1803)

Laws, as we read in ancient sages,
Have been like cobwebs in all ages.
Cobwebs for little flies are spread,
And laws for little folks are made;
But if an insect of renown,
Hornet or beetle, wasp or drone,
Be caught in quest of sport or plunder,
The flimsy fetter flies in sunder.[10]

"The Death of the Fly" by Johann Wolfgang von Goethe (1749–1832)

With eagerness he drinks the treach'rous potion,
    Nor stops to rest, by the first taste misled;
Sweet is the draught, but soon all pow'r of motion
    He finds has from his tender members fled;
No longer has he strength to plume his wing,
No longer strength to raise his head, poor thing!
E'en in enjoyment's hour his life he loses,
His little foot to bear his weight refuses;
So on he sips, and ere his draught is o'er
Death veils his thousand eyes for evermore.[11]

"On Finding a Small Fly Crushed in a Book" by Charles Tennyson Turner (1808–1879)

Some hand, that never meant to do thee hurt,
Has crushed thee here between these pages pent,
But thou has left thine own fair monument,
Thy wings gleam out and tell me what thou wert:
Oh! That the memories, which survive us here,
Were half as lovely as these wings of thine!
Pure relics of a blameless life, that shine
Now thou art gone: Our doom is ever near:
The peril is beside us, day by day;
The book will close upon us it may be,
Just as we lift ourselves to soar away
Upon the summer-airs. But unlike thee,
The closing book may stop our vital breath,
Yet leave no luster on our page of death.[12]

From "Our Old Feuillage" (from *Leaves of Grass*) by Walt Whitman (1819–1892)

Observing the spiral flight of two little yellow
butterflies shuffling between each other,
ascending high in the air,
The darting swallow, the destroyer of insects, the fall
traveler southward but returning northward early
in the spring,

The country boy at the close of the day driving the
    herd of cows and shouting to them as they loiter to
    browse by the road-side,
The city wharf, Boston, Philadelphia, Baltimore,
    Charleston, New Orleans, San Francisco,
The departing ships when the sailors heave at the capstan;
Evening—me in my room—the setting sun,
The setting summer sun shining in my open window,
    showing the swarm of flies, suspended, balancing
    in the air in the centre of the room, darting
    athwart, up and down, casting swift shadows in
    specks on the opposite wall where the shine is.[13]

"The Fly: A Rhyme for Children" by Theodore Tilton (1835–1907)

I.

    Baby Bye,
    Here's a Fly:
Let us watch him, you and I.
    How he crawls
    Up the walls—
    Yet he never falls!
I believe, with those six legs,
You and I could walk on eggs!
    There he goes,
    On his toes,
    Tickling Baby's nose!

II.

Spots of red
Dot his head:
Rainbows on his wings are spread!
That small speck
Is his neck;
See him nod and beck!
I can show you, if you choose,
Where to look to find his shoes:
Three small pairs
Made of hairs—
These he always wears.

III.

Black and brown
Is his gown;
He can wear it upside down!
It is laced
Round his waist;
I admire his taste.
Pretty as his clothes are made,
He will spoil them, I'm afraid,
If to-night
He gets sight
Of the candle-light!

IV.

In the sun
Webs are spun:
What if he gets into one!
When it rains
He complains
On the window-panes.
Tongues to talk have you and I:
God has given the little Fly
No such things;
So he sings
With his buzzing wings.

V.

He can eat
Bread and meat;
See his mouth between his feet!
On his back
Hangs a sack,
Like a peddler's pack.
Does the Baby understand?
Then the Fly shall kiss her hand!
Put a crumb
On her thumb:
Maybe he will come!

VI.

> Round and round,
> On the ground,

On the ceiling he is found.

> Catch him? No:
> Let him go:
> Never hurt him so!

Now you see his wings of silk
Drabbled in the Baby's milk!

> Fie, oh fie!
> Foolish Fly!
> How will he get dry?

VII.

> All wet flies
> Twist their thighs:

So they wipe their heads and eyes.

> Cats, you know,
> Wash just so:
> Then their whiskers grow.

Flies have hair too short to comb!
Flies go barehead out from home!

> But the Gnat
> Wears a hat:
> Do you laugh at that?

VIII.

    Flies can see
    More than we—
So how bright their eyes must be!
    Little Fly,
    Mind your eye—
    Spiders are nearby!
Now a secret let me tell:
Spiders will not treat you well!
    So I say
    Heed your way!
    Little Fly, good day![14]

"A Tear (A Triolet)" by Austin Dobson (1840–1921)

There's a tear in her eye,—
    Such a clear little jewel!
What *can* make her cry?
There's a tear in her eye.
"Puck has killed a big fly,—
    And it's *horribly* cruel;"
There's a tear in her eye,—
    Such a clear little jewel![15]

"The Fly" by Walter de la Mare (1873–1956)

How large unto the tiny fly
Must little things appear!—
A rosebud like a feather bed,
Its prickle like a spear;

A dewdrop like a looking-glass,
A hair like golden wire;
The smallest grain of mustard-seed
As fierce as coals of fire;

A loaf of bread, a lofty hill;
A wasp, a cruel leopard;
And specks of salt as bright to see
As lambkins to a shepherd.[16]

"The Spider and the Ghost of the Fly" by Vachel Lindsay (1879–1931)

Once I loved a spider
When I was born a fly,
A velvet-footed spider
With a gown of rainbow-dye.
She ate my wings and gloated.
She bound me with a hair.
She drove me to her parlor

Above her winding stair.
To educate young spiders
She took me all apart.
My ghost came back to haunt her.
I saw her eat my heart.[17]

"The Fly" by Carmen Bernos de Gasztold (1919–1995)

Lord,
shall I always go in black
for this life?
Fugitive from its tumult
on my transparent wings,
humming my prayers
and pausing weightless
on my thin legs,
I,
whom the world finds such a burden?
You have made me
stick to what lures me.
Yet, if I am caught
clinging there
don't let me die
like the poor useless
thing that I am.
        Amen.[18]

"The Last Fly" by David Dalton (1945–)

Little capuchin, your black gun-metal mandibles thinner
     than the thickness
of a minute hand on the face of a watch.
Your glassine wings; your fearful robes like the cassock of
     a hanging judge.
Your hieratic mask, a halo of sea-anemone spines.
Your pantocratic eyes curved to the shape of space itself.
Your speech slurred like a radio drunk on electricity—
a demonic buzz into which genealogies of words are
     collapsed.
Time has become viscous and thick like honey with the
     weight of Fall,
and you, too, like your own punctuation mark, have
     slowed down—
your movements now ponderous and pondered.
Gravity has stunned you.
Once a dancer of miraculous pirouettes, you no
longer leap into flight like a mad Russian ballet dancer.
That terrible whine of yours, once irritating, now
     poignant.
The epitome of melancholy on a window sill.
You were sixty-five million years old when Gilgamesh
     was written.
Go now, little speck, the Fly King awaits you in the
     sashes of the window.[19]

Notes

Prologue

1. See Carlo Rovelli, *Seven Brief Lessons on Physics* (New York: Riverhead, 2016), 17.

2. William Wordsworth, "Ode [Intimations of Immortality]," in *The New Oxford Book of Romantic Period Verse*, ed. Jerome J. McGann (Oxford: Oxford University Press, 1993), 269.

3. Henry Vaughan, "The Retreat," in *English Verse*, vol. 2, *Campion to the Ballads*, ed. W. Peacock (London: Oxford University Press, 1971), 410.

4. Thomas Traherne, *The Works of Thomas Traherne*, vol. 5, *Centuries of Meditations and Select Meditations*, ed. Jan Ross (Cambridge, MA: D. S. Brewer, 2013), 15. Traherne's spelling and capitalization have been modernized here and in all subsequent quotations from Traherne's writings.

5. Thomas Traherne, "Wonder," in *The Works of Thomas Traherne*, vol. 6, ed. Jan Ross (Cambridge, MA: D. S. Brewer, 2014), 90.

6. C. S. Lewis, *Surprised by Joy* (New York: Harcourt, Brace & World, 1955), 222.

7. Lewis, *Surprised by Joy*, 19.

8. Benjamin Franklin, *Writings: The Autobiography, Poor Richard's Almanack, Bagatelles, Pamphlets, Essays, and Letters* (New York: Library of America, 1987), 1494.

9. Franklin, *Writings*, 1232. How right Franklin was! Scientists have since determined that a fly's feet are ten million times more sensitive to sugar than the human tongue is.

10. Other scholars suggest that the Babylonians themselves may have considered flies to be deities and used the name *Beelzebub* even before the Jewish priests got hold of it.

11. Exodus 8:21 NIV.

12. By that count, the total number of bugs worldwide is around 900 quadrillion; that's 900 with fifteen zeroes after it. Recent scientific studies calculate that that number is beginning to decline precipitously—at the rate of about 2.5 percent each year—due to pesticides and climate change. Too few bugs would be a devastating plague every bit as serious as too many. No bugs would mean the end of much life on earth, including human life. More about this in chapter 4.

13. Isaiah 7:18–19. The flies and bees are most likely symbols for Israel's enemies.

14. Dante Alighieri, *The Divine Comedy of Dante Alighieri*, vol. 1, *Inferno*, trans. Robert M. Durling (New York: Oxford University Press, 1996), 57.

15. Jean-Paul Sartre, *No Exit and Three Other Plays* (New York: Vintage, 1958).

16. Some entomologists speculate that there could be as many as a million species of fly.

17. Peter Nickolls and Henry Disney, "Flies Discovered at Casey Station," *Australian Antarctic Magazine* 1 (Autumn 2001): https://

tinyurl.com/y262w39f. For a time, some scientists argued that flies only appeared in Antarctica recently, having accompanied humans, but fly fossils that long predate humans have been discovered on the continent.

18. Redi was also a noted poet, known primarily for his poem "Bacchus in Tuscany," which is a hymn of nearly a thousand lines dedicated to the region's wines. Nowhere in his poems, however, does he ever mention flies!

19. Ralph Waldo Emerson, "The Poet," in *Essays: Second Series* (Boston: James Munroe, 1844), 23.

Chapter 1: Existence

1. C. S. Lewis, *The Collected Letters of C. S. Lewis*, vol. 2, *Books, Broadcasts, and the War, 1931–1949*, ed. Walter Hooper (New York: HarperCollins, 2004), 505. Lewis thought it to be the most beautiful book "in prose, . . . excluding poetry," thus his qualifying "almost."

2. Thomas Merton, *The Road to Joy: Letters to New and Old Friends*, ed. Robert E. Daggy (New York: Farrar, Straus & Giroux, 1989), 62.

3. This was somewhat anachronistic on Joyce's part since the action of *Ulysses* takes place on June 16, 1904, four years before the publication of Traherne's *Centuries of Meditation*. The phrase is "orient and immortal," which occurs in chapters 3 and 10 of *Ulysses*.

4. Thomas Traherne, *The Works of Thomas Traherne*, vol. 1, *Inducements to Retirednes, A Sober View of Dr. Twisses his Considerations, Seeds of Eternity of the Nature of the Soul, The Kingdom of God*, ed. Jan Ross (Cambridge, MA: D. S. Brewer, 2005), 422–23. As in the prologue, Traherne's spelling and capitalization have been modernized throughout.

5. William Blake, "The Tyger," in *Songs of Innocence and of Experience*, facsimile, ed. Andrew Lincoln (Princeton, NJ: The William Blake Trust/Princeton University Press, 1991), plate 42.

6. In Traherne's time, according to the OED, the word *resentment* could mean a strong emotion of any kind, not just one of anger or affront.

7. Nick Page, *Lord Minimus* (New York: St. Martin's, 2002), 11.

8. 1 Corinthians 13:12.

9. 1 Corinthians 13:12 in Wycliffe's translation: "we seen now bi a myrour in derknesse."

10. Robert Hooke, *Micrographia: Or Some Physiological Descriptions of Minute Bodies Made by Magnifying Glasses with Observations and Inquiries Thereupon* (London: The Royal Society of London, 1665), 182, 184.

11. Thomas Traherne, *The Works of Thomas Traherne*, vol. 3, *Commentaries of Heaven, Part 2: Al-Sufficient to Bastard*, ed. Jan Ross (Cambridge, MA: D. S. Brewer, 2007), 318.

12. Galileus Galieus Linceus, *The Systeme of the World: In Four Dialogues—Wherein the Two Grand Systemes of Ptolemy and Copernicus Are Largely Discoursed of . . . Inglished from the Original Italian by Thomas Salusbury* (London: William Leybourne, 1661).

13. Thomas Aquinas, *Sermon-Conferences of St. Thomas Aquinas on the Apostles' Creed*, ed. Nicholas R. Ayo (Eugene, OR: Wipf & Stock, 1988), 21.

14. Traherne never mentions Aquinas in *The Roman Forgeries*, Traherne's rebuttal of Catholic theology, but a number of writers have noted his familiarity with Aquinas. See Gladys I. Wade, "St. Thomas Aquinas and Thomas Traherne," *New Blackfriars* 12, no. 140 (November 1931): 666–73; Paul Cefalu, "Thomistic Metaphysics and Ethics in the Prose and Poetry of Thomas Traherne," *Literature and Theology* 16, no. 3 (September 2002): 248–69; and K. W. Salter, *Thomas Traherne: Mystic and Poet* (New York: Barnes & Noble, 1965), 10, 34–36. Also, the previous quote from Aquinas is from his commentary on the Nicene Creed; since *The Roman Forgeries* was a critique of the creeds, it is possible that Traherne had read that commentary.

15. For more on Traherne's responses to Hobbes, see Kathryn Murphy, "Thomas Traherne, Thomas Hobbes, and the Rhetoric of Realism,"

The Seventeenth Century 28, no. 4 (2013): 419–39. Though not discussed here, Traherne would also have objected to Hobbes's materialism, which tended to view science as undermining our need for God. Traherne, of course, felt that science, as it advanced, could do nothing but teach us more about God's ways.

16. Thomas Hobbes, *Leviathan* (New York: Penguin, 1985 [1651]), 186.
17. G. K. Chesterton, "Tolstoy and the Cult of Simplicity," in *Varied Types* (New York: Dodd, Mead, 1905), 141.
18. Traherne, *Works*, 3:93.
19. Traherne, *Works*, 3:333.
20. Hebrews 2:6–7.
21. William Blake, "Auguries of Innocence," in *Blake: Complete Writings with Variant Readings*, ed. Geoffrey Keynes (London: Oxford University Press, 1972), 431.
22. Traherne, *Works*, 5:11.
23. Traherne, *Works*, 3:323.
24. Eleanor Farjeon, "Morning Has Broken," in *Songs of Praise*, ed. Percy Dreamer, Ralph Vaughan Williams, and Martin Shaw (London: Oxford University Press, 1931), 31, hymn 30.
25. Traherne, *Works*, 5:16.

Chapter 2: Mortality

1. Our time traveler is more likely to encounter playwright John Gay, who was also a member of the Scriblerus Club. Swift never returned to England after 1727.
2. This earliest known version appeared as "The Fly: An Anacreontick" in *The Scarborough Miscellany for the Year 1732, Consisting of Original Poems, Tales, Songs, Epigrams, etc.* (London: J. Roberts, 1732). With minor word changes, later versions divided the poem into three stanzas of four lines each, which was probably done to facilitate being set to music. It is unclear whether the original version is intended to be one twelve-line poem or a poem of two six-line stanzas, since the

poem is broken over two pages halfway through. I have set it without any stanza breaks since Oldys's models, Stanley and Cowley, never broke their Anacreontic poetry into stanzas.

3. Joseph Ritson, ed., *Select Collection of English Songs in Three Volumes, Volume the Second* (London: J. Johnson in St. Paul's Churchyard, 1783), 17. The song was originally written for two voices and published in London as a broadsheet in 1640.

4. Oldys might have written "The Fly" earlier, while living in Yorkshire, though it was first published in 1732, two years after he moved to London.

5. Isaac D'Israeli, *Curiosities of Literature* (London: George Routledge & Sons, 1866), 566.

6. The poem appears in, among many others, A. T. Quiller-Couch, ed., *Oxford Book of English Verse 1250–1900* (1901); David Nichol Smith, ed., *The Oxford Book of Eighteenth Century Verse* (1926); W. J. Turner, ed., *Eighteenth Century Poetry* (1931); John Wain, ed., *The Oxford Anthology of English Poetry*, vol. 1 (1990); Christopher Ricks, ed., *The Oxford Book of English Verse* (1999); Dorothy Belle Pollack, ed., *Great Short Poems from Antiquity to the Twentieth Century* (2011).

7. See James Yeowell and William Oldys, *A Literary Antiquary: Memoir of William Oldys, Esq. . . .* (London: Spottiswoode, 1862), xii–xiii. It was common at that time for poetry to be published without attribution. Scottish writer Charles Mackay, in his *Songs of England* ([London: Houlston & Wright, n.d.], 130) says that "some authorities" attribute the poem to neo-Latin poet Vincent Bourne (1695–1747), though he notes that others attribute it to Oldys.

8. Yeowell lists a "Collection of Poems by Mr. Oldys" among the author's unpublished manuscripts (*Literary Antiquary*, xlix). To my knowledge, other than a few epigrams, Oldys's other poems have never appeared in print.

9. Anacreon's surviving poetry is fragmentary, but a group of about sixty poems—now called the *Anacreontea*—by ancient imitators of Anacreon were mistakenly accepted as his originals. These were the

poems adapted by Stanley and Cowley. Poet Robert Herrick also adapted a few of his own around that time.

10. These poems comprised one section of the "Miscellanies" in Abraham Cowley, *Poems* (London: Humphrey Moseley, 1656). Cowley considered them juvenilia, so his versions probably predate Stanley's. Some of these adaptations were further edited and later reprinted by Francis Willis, *Anacreon Done into English out of the Original Greek* (Oxford: 1683).

11. Horace, *Odes*, 1.11.8. *Carpe diem* is sometimes also translated as "seize the present" and "pluck the moment."

12. Translated by Miriam Lichtheim in *The Context of Scripture: Monumental Inscriptions from the Biblical World*, vol. 2, ed. William W. Hallo and K. Lawson Younger (Leiden: Brill, 1997), 65. The pharaoh was Intef I.

13. Ecclesiastes 8:15.

14. 1 Corinthians 15:32.

15. Robert Herrick, "To the Virgins, to Make Much of Time," in *The Poems of Robert Herrick* (London: Oxford University Press, 1933), 88.

16. Samuel Johnson, *The Latin Poems*, ed. Niall Rudd (Lewisburg, PA: Bucknell University Press, 2005), 60. Italics added. The English translation is my own.

17. Pliny the Elder, in his *Natural History* (vii.7), reports that Anacreon choked to death on a grape seed, a claim doubted by modern scholars.

18. Cowley, "Elegie Upon Anacreon, Who Was Choked by a Grape-Stone," in *Poems*, 39. All italics in Cowley's poems are in the original.

19. Cowley, "The Grasshopper," in *Poems*, 37. Stanley also adapted an Anacreontic "Grasshopper" poem, but in his version, the grasshopper sips the dew with no reference to wine.

20. D'Israeli, *Curiosities*, 560–61.

21. Bolton Corney, *Curiosities of Literature by Isaac D'Israeli Illustrated* (London: Richard Bentley, 1838), 182. The portion in single quotes is Corney quoting D'Israeli, *Curiosities*, 566.

22. D'Israeli (*Curiosities*, 559) writes that later in Oldys's life, his "deep potations of ale" became a "prevalent infirmity." A story circulated that Oldys was drunk while participating in his official capacity at a royal wedding. Corney (*Curiosities*, 167) disputes all this as slander and hearsay.

23. Ecclesiastes 12:12.

24. Isaac D'Israeli, quoted in R. Chambers, ed., *The Book of Days: A Miscellany of Popular Antiquities*, vol. 1 (Edinburgh: W&R Chambers, 1863), 514. Chambers gives no source, but the quotation is not from D'Israeli's *Curiosities of Literature*.

25. D'Israeli, *Curiosities*, 563.

26. Abraham Cowley, "Of Solitude," in *The Works of Abraham Cowley*, 5th. ed. (London: Henry Herringman, 1678), 92.

27. Corney, *Curiosities*, 166.

28. In 1753, the British government purchased Harley's magnificent collection, which is now housed in the British Library.

29. Roger L'Estrange, ed., *Seneca's Morals by Way of Abstract* (Edinburgh: Martin & Sons, 1776), 173. L'Estrange's translation was first published in 1693, though the edition in Harley's library was from 1722.

30. Seneca, "De Brevitate Vitae," *Moral Essays*, vol. 2, Loeb Classical Library (Cambridge, MA: Harvard University Press, 1990), 327.

31. Seneca, "De Brevitate Vitae," 339.

32. From Sam Hamill's introduction to Kobayashi Issa, *The Spring of My Life and Selected Haiku*, trans. Sam Hamill (Boston: Shambhala, 1997), xii.

33. Yeowell and Oldys, *A Literary Antiquary*, xxxix.

Chapter 3: Imagination

1. Henry Alfred Burd, *Joseph Ritson: A Critical Biography* (Urbana: University of Illinois Press, 1916), 91.

2. Ritson, *Select Collection of English Songs*.

3. Stothard was not the only artist whose artwork was included in the book, but he provided most of the pieces—eight in all. Swiss artist Henry Fuseli, a friend to both Stothard and Blake at the Royal Academy, provided a frontispiece illustration, which was engraved by James Heath. It also seems as if Fuseli first recommended Blake to Ritson and Johnson.

4. Color printing by means of multiple plates was also done at the time—a process called aquatint—but it was most often used for stand-alone pictures to be hung on the wall rather than printed in books.

5. The friend was Seymour Kirkup, quoted in Harold Bloom and Alexis Harley, eds., *Bloom's Classic Critical Views: William Blake* (New York: Infobase Publishing, 2008), 24.

6. Walt Whitman, *Walt Whitman Speaks*, ed. Brenda Wineapple (New York: Library of America, 2019), 27.

7. Blake's books may be rarer, but they're not as expensive. At auction, a Shakespeare first folio, due to its age and reputation, will command about twice what a Blake illuminated book will. A first folio will sell for about $5 million, whereas the most recent copy of Blake's *First Book of Urizen* sold for $2.5 million.

8. Alexander Gilchrist, *Life of William Blake, "Pictor Ignotus"* (London: Macmillan, 1863), 2. Italics added.

9. Gilchrist, *Life*, 342.

10. Gilchrist, *Life*, 7. Gilchrist says Blake was "eight or ten."

11. Gilchrist, *Life*, 18.

12. Gilchrist, *Life*, 313.

13. William Blake, "To the Public," in *Jerusalem: The Emanation of the Giant Albion*, facsimile, ed. Morton D. Paley (Princeton, NJ: The William Blake Trust/Princeton University Press, 1991), plate 3.

14. William Blake, *Poetical Sketches*, facsimile (London: Tate Publishing, 2007), 15, 18. This edition is a facsimile of one of two copies apparently corrected in Blake's hand.

15. Blake engraved a couple of isolated plates for Johnson in the months before engraving the eight plates for Ritson's *Select Collection of*

English Songs, but Ritson's project was Blake's most extensive commission from Johnson to date. In the years that followed, Blake would do more than ninety additional commissions for Johnson.

16. Ritson, *Select Collection of English Songs*, 17. The poem itself spans pages 17–18. Ritson reproduced Greene's musical setting for the song as "Song XIX. Busy curious thirsty fly. Set by dr. Greene" in volume 3 of *A Select Collection of English Songs* (the pages are unnumbered).

17. David V. Erdman and Donald K. Moore, eds., *The Notebook of William Blake: A Photographic and Typographic Facsimile* (London: Oxford University Press, 1973), transcript and plate N101.

18. William Blake, *The Marriage of Heaven and Hell*, facsimile (London: Oxford University Press, 1975), plates 7.

19. Emanuel Swedenborg, *The Wisdom of Angels Concerning Divine Love and Divine Wisdom*, trans. Nathaniel Tucker (London: W. Chalklen, 1788), 326–27. This is the translation that Blake read. Swedenborg's original was written in Latin and published in Amsterdam in 1763.

20. William Shakespeare, *King Lear*, 4.1.38–39.

21. James Hervey, *Meditations and Contemplations* (London: John & James Rivington, 1748), 21. The internal quotation is a reference to Job 4:19: "How much less *in* them that dwell in houses of clay, whose foundation *is* in the dust, *which* are crushed before the moth." Hervey admits in a footnote that his own translation of this verse is extremely idiosyncratic.

22. In the third chapter of his illuminated book *Jerusalem: The Emanation of the Giant Albion*, Blake lists Hervey as one of the guardians of the Gates of Los, alongside four of Blake's other favorite writers: poet and theologian François Fénelon, mystics Madame Guyon and Teresa of Ávila, and Methodist evangelist George Whitefield— "with all the gentle Souls / Who guide the great Wine-press of Love" (plate 72, lines 50–52).

23. Ritson, "Song LVIII," in *Selection Collection of English Songs*, 164–65.

24. Blake, *Songs of Innocence*, plates 42 and 8. "The Fly" is plate 40.

25. A few scholars suggest that Blake's fly is actually a butterfly. One of the more convincing arguments is the small V-shaped mark next to

the final line of the poem. Is it a butterfly or part of a tree branch? Still, I believe the clear connection to Oldys's poem throws the argument in favor of taking Blake at face value, and most scholars accept that by *fly*, Blake meant a *fly*. Though see S. Foster Damon, *A Blake Dictionary: The Ideas and Symbols of William Blake* (Hanover, NH: University Press of New England, 1988), 139–40. Whether a fly or butterfly is intended does not affect the themes of thought, imagination, and vision presented in this chapter.

26. This image is taken from Edwin J. Ellis, ed., *Facsimile of the Original Outlines before Coloring of* The Songs of Innocence and of Experience *Executed by William Blake* (London: Bernard Quaritch, 1893), 40. Blake's original was printed in a reddish brown ink.

27. William Blake, *Milton a Poem*, facsimile, ed. Robert N. Essick and Joseph Viscomi (Princeton, NJ: The William Blake Trust/Princeton University Press, 1995) plate 32*(e).

28. Blake, *Marriage of Heaven and Hell*, plates 23–24.

29. Blake, "To Thomas Butts, 22 November 1802," in *Complete Writings*, 815.

30. Blake, *Jerusalem*, plate 77.

31. Blake, *Marriage of Heaven and Hell*, plate 30.

32. Blake, "To Rev. Trusler, August 23, 1799," in *Complete Writings*, 793–94.

33. Matthew 7:13.

34. Blake, "Mock on, Mock on Voltaire, Rousseau," in *Complete Writings*, 418.

35. Blake, "Laocoön," in *Complete Writings*, 777.

36. Blake, *Marriage of Heaven and Hell*, plate 8.

37. Blake, *Jerusalem*, plate 77.

38. Blake, "London," in *Songs of Innocence*, plate 46.

39. Blake, "Laocoön," in *Complete Writings*, 776.

40. Malcolm Muggeridge, *The Third Testament* (Boston: Little, Brown, 1976), 90.

41. Joseph Ritson, *Robin Hood: A Collection of All the Ancient Poems, Songs, and Ballads, Now Extant, Relative to that Celebrated English*

Outlaw: To Which Are Prefixed Historical Anecdotes of His Life, 2 vols. (London: T. Egerton, 1795), 1:xl.

42. Gilchrist, *Life*, 361.
43. Gilchrist, *Life*, 362.
44. William Blake, "A Memorable Fancy," in *Marriage of Heaven and Hell*, plate 12.

Chapter 4: Compassion

1. Robert Bly, "About Issa," in *Ten Poems by Issa: English Versions by Robert Bly*, ed. Robert Bly, illus. Arthur Okamura (Point Reyes Station, CA: Floating Island, 1992), n.p. Bly's full quotation: "He is the greatest haiku poet of the 19th century, the greatest frog poet in the world, the greatest fly poet in the world, and maybe the greatest child poet in the world."
2. The haiku in this chapter were translated by Asano Karasu and used with permission. Note that like most contemporary English translations of Japanese haiku, these attempt to be dynamic renderings and do not conform to the five-seven-five syllable structure.
3. Makoto Ueda, *Dew on the Grass: The Life and Poetry of Kobayashi Issa* (Boston: Brill, 2004), 22.
4. Ueda, *Dew on the Grass*, 9–10.
5. Matsuo Bashō's *Oku no Hosomichi* (*Narrow Road to the Deep North*) was first published in 1702.
6. Issa wrote this haiku as part of his notebook entitled *Hachiban Nikki* ("The Eighth Diary").
7. 1 John 4:8.
8. Mark 12:30–31.
9. Luke 10:33.
10. Matthew 9:36, 15:32; Luke 7:13; Mark 9:22, 25, respectively.
11. Francisco Sánchez-Bayo and Kris A. G. Wyckhuys, "Worldwide Decline of Entomofauna: A Review of Its Drivers" *Biological Conservation* 232 (April 2019): 8–27, doi.org/10.1016/j.biocon.2019.01.020.

12. For instance, see Ed Yong, "Is the Insect Apocalypse Really Upon Us?" *The Atlantic*, February 19, 2019, https://tinyurl.com/y6jnrxd9. I would also like to thank Dr. David Dornbos, professor of biology at Calvin University, for hashing over the ideas in this section with me.

13. Floyd W. Shockley quoted in "Ask Smithsonian," *Smithsonian* 50, no. 1 (April 2019): 84.

14. "Media Release: Nature's Dangerous Decline 'Unprecedented'; Species Extinction Rates 'Accelerating,'" *IPBES Science and Policy for People and Nature*, May 2019, https://tinyurl.com/y4qv72ud.

15. Kobayashi Issa, *The Spring of My Life and Selected Haiku*, trans. Sam Hamill (Boston: Shambhala, 1997), 60.

16. Matthew 25:40.

Chapter 5: The Soul

1. Pierpont's gravestone can be seen at https://digitalheritage.noblenet .org/wakefield/items/show/1558.

2. Bull's gravestone can be seen at https://www.findagrave.com /memorial/11290182/esther-bull.

3. Thanks to Dr. Kevin Corcoran, professor of philosophy at Calvin University, for inspiring the tombstone illustration. When I accompanied him on his visiting lectureship at Xiamen University, Xiamen, China, in 2004, he would sometimes begin his lectures on the nature of the soul by describing gravestones similar to the ones I have described here. He used the gravestones to illustrate the two contrasting views of the soul in early American religion. For a thorough and detailed account of Corcoran's "philosophy of persons," see his excellent book, *Rethinking Human Nature: A Christian Materialist Alternative to the Soul* (Grand Rapids: Baker, 2006).

4. I know many would disagree with my assessment, and I would qualify my own statement by saying that Walt Whitman was every bit as original, profound, and influential as Dickinson. More than any

two American poets, they established a national poetic voice, unbe-holden to European models. In my opinion, Dickinson and Whit-man (to borrow Eliot's phrase) divide the world between them. There is no third.

5. Emily Dickinson, "I felt a Funeral, in my Brain," in *Emily Dickinson's Poems: As She Preserved Them*, ed. Cristanne Miller (Cambridge, MA: Belknap Press, 2016), 179.

6. Edward Young, "Night Thoughts," in *English Verse*, vol. 3, *Dryden to Wordsworth*, ed. W. Peacock (London: Oxford University Press, 1972), 107.

7. This last phrase in single quotation marks is from a lengthy narrative poem, "Marco Bazzaris" (1825), by a popular American poet at that time, Fitz-Greene Halleck. He was sometimes called "the American Byron."

8. Ralph Waldo Emerson, "Threnody," in *Poems* (Boston: James Monroe, 1847), 248.

9. J. B. Aikin, *The Christian Minstrel* (Philadelphia: T. K. Collins, 1858), 210, 37. This hymnal, first published in 1846, was one of the most widely used in the singing schools of the 1840s and 1850s.

10. Dickinson, "They dropped like Flakes," in *Emily Dickinson's Poems*, 298.

11. Dickinson, "It feels a shame to be Alive," in *Emily Dickinson's Poems*, 257.

12. Dickinson, "I heard a Fly buzz," in *Emily Dickinson's Poems*, 270.

13. Common meter is also called "ballad form" and originated with the early English ballads. Dickinson was familiar with both the ballads and the hymns but drew more inspiration from the latter.

14. Edwards A. Park, Austin Phelps, and Lowell Mason, eds., *The Sabbath Hymn Book for the Service of Song in the House of the Lord* (New York: Mason Brothers, 1858), 273, hymns 1196 and 1197.

15. Park, Phelps, and Mason, *Sabbath Hymn Book*, 101, 103, hymns 423, 431, and 432.

16. William B. O. Peabody (1799–1847), "Behold, the Western Evening Light," in *Sabbath Hymn Book*, 274, hymn 1199. Peabody's hymn was first published in 1823.

17. Coincidentally, when John Newton's words for "Amazing Grace" were first paired in print with its now inseparable tune, called "New Britain," it was in the key of F—in William Walker's shape-note hymnal *Southern Harmony* (1835), 85. It was later transposed to the key of G, in which it is most often sung today.

18. Dickinson, "How many times these low feet staggered," in *Emily Dickinson's Poems*, 104.

19. Dickinson, "Some – keep the Sabbath – going to church," in *Emily Dickinson's Poems*, 115.

20. Dickinson, "I prayed, at first, a little Girl," in *Emily Dickinson's Poems*, 298.

21. Dickinson, "I know that He exists," in *Emily Dickinson's Poems*, 193.

22. Emily Dickinson, *The Letters of Emily Dickinson*, vol. 1, ed. Mabel Loomis Todd (Boston: Little, Brown, 1906), 302. See also Emily Dickinson, *Selected Letters*, ed. Thomas H. Johnson (Cambridge, MA: Belknap Press, 1986), 172. The letter is dated April 25, 1862.

23. Luke 16:22–23.

24. Dickinson, "A long – long Sleep," in *Emily Dickinson's Poems*, 232.

25. Dickinson, "Because I could not stop for Death," in *Emily Dickinson's Poems*, 239.

26. Dickinson, "I never saw a Moor," in *Emily Dickinson's Poems*, 532. The word *Checks* means "train ticket."

27. Dickinson, "Heaven is so far of the Mind," in *Emily Dickinson's Poems*, 220.

28. Dickinson, "'Heaven' is what I cannot reach!" and "Why – do they shut Me out of Heaven," in *Emily Dickinson's Poems*, 162, 133.

29. Dickinson, *Selected Letters*, 279. Letter dated April 30, 1882.

30. James McIntosh, *Nimble Believing: Dickinson and the Unknown* (Ann Arbor: University of Michigan Press, 2000), 1.

31. Mark 9:24.

32. Czeslaw Milosz, "Treatise on Theology," in *Second Space: New Poems*, trans. Czeslaw Milosz and Robert Haas (New York: HarperCollins, 2004), 63.

33. Dickinson, "Their Hight in Heaven comforts not," in *Emily Dickinson's Poems*, 363.

34. Dickinson, *Selected Letters*, 330.
35. My wife and I visited Dickinson's grave on October 23, 2019. We also visited the Emily Dickinson Museum in the Homestead. There we saw her bedroom, with its south- and west-facing windows, which, in summer, would have attracted flies trying to reach the afternoon sunlight.

Chapter 6: Things

1. James Boswell, *The Life of Samuel Johnson*, vol. 1 (London: Dent, 1906 [1791]), 292.
2. Steve Gagnon, "Questions and Answers: How Much of an Atom Is Empty Space," *Jefferson Lab*, https://tinyurl.com/y4all9hj.
3. William Shakespeare, *Hamlet*, 1.5.167–68.
4. Donald D. Hoffman, *The Case against Reality: Why Evolution Hid the Truth from Our Eyes* (New York: W. W. Norton, 2019).
5. Donald D. Hoffman, quoted in Tim Folger, "Your Daily Dose of Quantum: How the Science of the Super Small Lets You Smell, See, Touch and More," *Discover* 39, no 9 (November 2018): 36–37.
6. Guillaume Apollinaire, "Cubism," from *The Cubist Painters*, in *Modernism: An Anthology of Sources and Documents*, ed. Vassiliki Kolocotroni, Jane Goldman, and Olga Taxidou (Chicago: University of Chicago Press, 1998), 264.
7. Apparently, Cocteau is the one who urged Satie to insert those instruments, an idea that Satie at first rejected.
8. Guillaume Apollinaire, *Selected Writings*, trans. Roger Shattuck (New York: New Directions, 1971), 237.
9. Apollinaire, *Selected Writings*, 235.
10. Apollinaire, *Selected Writings*, 232. Italics in original.
11. These eighteen pieces were published as "La Marchande des quatre saisons ou le bestiaire mondain" in *La Phalange* (June 15, 1908).
12. Guillaume Apollinaire, *Alcools suivi de Le Bestiaire* (Paris: Gallimard, 1920), 160, 155, 156, and 158 (flea, mouse, elephant, and caterpillar, respectively). All English translations of poems from *Le Bestiaire* are

by C. Matin, 2019, from an unpublished manuscript and are used with permission.

13. Apollinaire, *Alcools*, 159. Here is the poem in the original French:

> Nos mouches savent des chansons
> Que leur apprirent en Norvège
> Les mouches ganiques qui sont
> Les divinités de la neige.

14. Joseph [Giuseppe] Acerbi, *Travels through Sweden, Finland, and Lapland, and to the North Cape in the Years 1798 and 1799*, vol. 2 (London: Joseph Mawman, 1802), 311. Italics in the original.

15. R. Raynal, "Qu'est ce que . . . 'le Cubisme'?" *Comœdia illustré*, December 20, 1913, quoted in Edward F. Fry, *Cubism* (New York: McGraw-Hill, 1966), 129–30.

16. Pablo Picasso, "Picasso Speaks," in *The Arts* (New York: The Arts Publishing Corporation, 1923), n.p.

17. Blake, *Jerusalem*, plate 77.

18. Apollinaire, in Kolocotroni, Goldman, and Taxidou, *Modernism*, 263.

19. Apollinaire, *Alcools*, 157.

20. Gertrude Stein, "Sacred Emily," in *Geography and Plays* (Boston: Four Seas, 1922), 187.

21. Gertrude Stein, "Poetry and Grammar," in *Toward the Open Field: Poets on the Art of Poetry, 1800–1950*, ed. Melizza Kwazny (Middletown, CT: Wesleyan University Press, 2003), 303. Stein wrote this essay in 1933.

22. William Wordsworth, "Ode [Intimations of Immortality]," in McGann, *New Oxford Book of Romantic Period Verse*, 269.

23. Henry Vaughan, "The Retreat," in Peacock, *English Verse*, 2:410.

24. Lewis, *Surprised by Joy*, 222.

25. Folger, "Daily Dose of Quantum," 37.

26. Shelley Townsend-Hudson, "Baby in a Car, 1956," in *When I Got Drunk with My Mother* (Ada, MI: Perkipery, 2019), 12.

27. Apollinaire, *Alcools*, 145.

28. Owen Barfield, *Poetic Diction: A Study in Meaning* (Middletown, CT: Wesleyan University Press, 1973), 171.
29. Apollinaire, in Kolocotroni, Goldman, and Taxidou, *Modernism*, 265.
30. Apollinaire, *Alcools*, 168.
31. Apollinaire, *Alcools*, 178.

Chapter 7: Story

1. Donagh MacDonagh and Lennox Robinson, eds., *The Oxford Book of Irish Verse, XVIIth Century–XXth Century* (London: Oxford University Press, 1958), 255–56.
2. Robert Farren, "The Pets," in *This Man Was Ireland: The Song of Colmcille, the Exile: A Poem* (New York: Sheed & Ward, 1943), 117–18.
3. Robert Farren, "School Teacher," in *Selected Poems* (London: Sheed & Ward, 1951), 170–71.
4. Farren's *The First Exile* was simultaneously published in the United States under the title *This Man Was Ireland*. The US edition is referenced in this chapter.
5. Farren, "O Father Colm was Gentle," in *This Man Was Ireland*, 122.
6. Adamnan, *Prophecies, Miracles and Visions of St. Columba (Columcille)*, trans. J. T. Fowler (London: Henry Frowde, 1895), 25.
7. As harsh as the king's judgment may seem, it anticipates modern copyright law: the owner of a book's content has the right to decide who can and can't copy that content.
8. Farren, "The Battle of Cooldrevny," in *This Man Was Ireland*, 86.
9. This story and photos of Columba's Psalter may be found at "The Cathach/The Psalter of Saint Columba," *Royal Irish Academy*, July 2, 2014, https://tinyurl.com/y238n8h8. The extant leaves contain Psalms 30:10–105:13 and constitute about half of the original manuscript. The other half is presumably lost.
10. Saint Colm, "Adiutor laborantium" (The Helper of Workers), in *The Edinburgh History of Scottish Literature*, vol. 1, *From Columba to the*

Union (until 1707), ed. Thomas Owen Clancy, Murray Pittock, Ian Brown, and Susan Manning (Edinburgh: Edinburgh University Press, 2007), 95. The translation from Latin is my own.

11. This woodcut is from Alfred Rimmer, *Ancient Stone Crosses of England* (London: Virtue, Spaulding, 1875), 90. The high-resolution image was kindly provided by Karen Hatzigeorgiou from her website Karen's Whimsy.

12. Manus O'Donnell, *Betha Colaim Chille: Life of Columcille*, trans. A. O'Kelleher and G. Schoepperle (Urbana: University of Illinois, 1918), 111, 113.

13. Alexander Carmichael, *Carmina Gadelica: Hymns and Incantations*, vol. 1 (Edinburgh: T&A Constable, 1900), 11. This is just one stanza of a much longer invocation of the nine graces of God. This was collected from a Scottish woman named Catherine Macauley in the early years of the nineteenth century.

14. 1 Corinthians 15:26.

15. J. R. R. Tolkien, "On Fairy-Stories," in *The Monsters and the Critics and Other Essays* (Boston: Houghton Mifflin, 1983), 153.

16. O'Donnell, *Betha Colaim Chille*, xxix–xxx.

17. Matthew 5:5.

18. George Herbert, "Grace," in *The Poems of George Herbert* (London: Oxford University Press, 1974), 52.

19. Psalm 90:9.

20. Tolkien, *Monsters and the Critics*, 156.

21. John 20:19.

Epilogue

1. Mike McClintock, *A Fly Went By*, illus. Fritz Siebel (New York: Random House, 1958).

2. Lucian, "[In Praise of] The Fly, *Musca Laudatio*," in *Lucian*, trans. A. M. Harmon (London: William Heinemann, 1913), 95. I have broken the lines into verse.

Appendix

1. According to Lucian, *The Works of Lucian of Samosata*, trans. H. W. Fowler and F. G. Fowler (Adelaide: University of Adelaide, 2014), ch. 50, https://tinyurl.com/y36ypx2w.
2. The Greek version of Simonides's "Dirge" can be found in C. M. Bowra, *Greek Lyric Poetry from Alcman to Simonides* (Oxford: Oxford University Press, 1961), 324. The translation is my own. Simonides is quite likely referring to a dragonfly.
3. William Shakespeare, *Titus Andronicus*, act 3, scene 2, The Arden Shakespeare (London: Methuen, 1961), 72–73.
4. Herrick, "The Amber Bead," in *Poems*, 286. Capitalization and spelling have been modernized.
5. Herbert, "Complaining," in *Poems*, 134. Spelling modernized. At least one scholar has speculated that Blake, in writing "The Fly," may have known this poem of Herbert's, especially in reference to Herbert's line "I a silly fly / That live or die."
6. Jean de La Fontaine, "The Coach and the Ant," in *The Fables of la Fontaine*, trans. E. Wright (London: Ingram, Cooke, 1853), 43. Capitalization and spelling have been modernized.
7. Matsuo Bashō, haiku "uki hito no." Unpublished translation by Asano Karasu. Used with permission.
8. Hattori Ransetsu, haiku. Unpublished translation by Asano Karasu. Used with permission. Ransetsu was one of Bashō's most devoted disciples. This whimsical haiku anticipates the poetry of Issa.
9. Thomas Gray, "The Ode on Spring," in *The New Oxford Book of Eighteenth Century Verse*, ed. Roger Lonsdale (Oxford: Oxford University Press, 1984), 349–50. Gray's "Brushed by the hand of rough Mischance" anticipates Blake's "Till some blind hand / Shall brush my wing" ("The Fly").
10. This verse is the opening stanza of James Beattie's "The Wolf and Shepherds: A Fable," in *The Poetical Works of James Beattie* (London: William Pickering, 1831), 141.

11. Johann Wolfgang von Goethe, *The Poems of Goethe*, trans. Edgar Alfred Bowring (London: Parker & Son, 1853), 306. Goethe wrote this poem in 1810. Goethe was not exaggerating. Each of the common housefly's two eyes contains more than four thousand individual lenses.

12. Charles Tennyson Turner, *Collected Sonnets Old and New* (London: C. Kegan Paul, 1880), 308. Turner was Lord Tennyson's elder brother. He specialized in sonnet writing and wrote more than three hundred of them in his lifetime. Spelling modernized.

13. Walt Whitman, "Our Old Feuillage," from *Leaves of Grass*, 1891–1892, in Walt Whitman, *Poetry and Prose* (New York: Library of America, 1982), 321–22.

14. Theodore Tilton, *The Sexton's Tale and Other Poems* (New York: Sheldon, 1867), 163–69. The original publisher includes this footnote to Tilton's poem: "These lines have been set to music by Lowell Mason; they may be sung also to the tune of 'Lightly Row.'"

15. Austin Dobson, "A Tear (A Triolet)," *Old-World Idylls and Other Verses* (London: Kegan Paul, Trench, Trübner, 1893), 212.

16. Walter de la Mare, *A Choice of de la Mare's Verse*, ed. W. H. Auden (London: Faber & Faber, 1963), 37.

17. Vachel Lindsay, *The Congo and Other Poems* (New York: Macmillan, 1915), 99–100.

18. From Carmen Bernos de Gasztold, *The Creatures' Choir*, trans. Rumer Godden (New York: Viking, 1965), 55.

19. David Dalton, "The Last Fly," unpublished poem. Copyright © 2020 by David Dalton. Used with permission.

Acknowledgments

This book began as a blog entry at the now-defunct Working-POET website in 2004. It would never have become a book without the help of the following people, whom I would like to thank:

- Tim Beals of Credo Communications, a consummate bookman and scholar.
- Emily Brower, acquisitions editor at Broadleaf Books, whose editorial guidance improved this book one hundred percent.
- Copy editor Allyce Amidon, whose sharp eye saved me from many embarrassing mistakes, and production editor Claire Vanden Branden.

- Proofreader Alyssa Lochner.
- The interior compositor: PerfecType Typesetting.
- Emily Benz, Mallory Hayes, and the Broadleaf Books marketing team.
- The Reverend Todd Petty of First Park Congregational Church of Grand Rapids, Michigan, for his wisdom on the subjects of faith and mystery.
- Dr. David Dornbos of the Au Sable Institute and professor and chair of the Biology Department of Calvin University, for explaining to me the perilous state of our biosphere, as discussed in the chapter about Kobayashi Issa.
- Dr. Kevin Corcoran, professor of philosophy at Calvin University, for our many discussions about the nature of the soul as we traveled through China.
- Philip C. Maurer of the University of Massachusetts, Amherst, for suggesting some helpful additions to the Emily Dickinson chapter.
- Brian Phipps, poet and senior editor at Zondervan; Emily Van Houten, publishing coordinator and manager of author care at Discovery House; Miranda Gardner, public relations manager at Brilliance Audio/Amazon Publishing; Kathleen Merz, acquisitions and managing editor at Eerdmans Books for Young People; and Dr. Michael P. Webster, professor of English at Grand Valley State University—all of whom challenged me and gave me patient feedback as

I discussed with them many of the ideas contained in this book. Thank you all for your friendship.

- Dr. Nancy Erickson, adjunct instructor at Asbury Theological Seminary and senior editor at Zondervan, who helped me with the Hebrew words and references; and Dr. Christopher Beetham, senior editor, biblical languages, textbooks, and reference tools for Zondervan Academic, who checked my Latin.

- Dr. Jennifer Holberg, professor of English at Calvin University and the codirector of the Calvin Center for Faith and Writing, and Dr. Jane Zwart, professor of English at Calvin University and codirector, with Dr. Holberg, of the Calvin Center for Faith and Writing, for their expertise and helpful, practical support.

- Dr. John T. Kirby, professor of classics at the University of Miami, who has an almost miraculous knack for affirming and encouraging. Every writer has an image of the ideal reader in the back of their mind, and John is mine.

- Linda Lambert, instructional services and collection development librarian at Taylor University, for her steadfast encouragement and for reading so much of my writing in manuscript.

- Author and poet David Dalton for his friendship and for granting permission to use his poem in the anthology.

- Jeff Morgan of the Emily Dickinson Museum, for his insights into the poet's life.
- Dr. Jan Ross, who generously shared a galley of her edition of Thomas Traherne's *Roman Forgeries* in advance of its publication as volume 7 of *The Works of Thomas Traherne*. Dr. Ross's work is a monument to exacting scholarship.
- The staffs at the Hekman Library at Calvin University, Grand Rapids, Michigan, and the Gramley Library at Salem College, Winston-Salem, North Carolina.

I'd also like to express my appreciation to:

- The Belknap Press of Harvard University Press, for their permission to quote Emily Dickinson's poems "as she preserved them."
- The Emily Dickinson Collection, Amherst College Archives & Special Collections, for permission to reproduce the page from Dickinson's own handwritten fascicles.
- Random House Children's Books, a division of Penguin Random House LLC, for their permission to reproduce

one of Fritz Siebel's drawings from Mike McClintock's *A Fly Went By.*

- Asano Karasu, who is closer than a brother to me, for providing the translations of Japanese haiku.
- Karen Hatzigeorgiou of Karen's Whimsy (karenswhimsey .com) for allowing me to draw from her amazing collection of rare, old images.
- Curtis Brown, Ltd., for permission to reprint "The Fly" from Carmen Bernos de Gasztold's *The Creatures' Choir*, translated by Rumer Godden.

Finally, I'd like to thank all those libraries worldwide for sharing digitized copies of the rare books in their collections. It's hard to express how grateful I am to live in an age when I can access on my computer thousands of books originally published centuries ago. William Oldys would be stunned. I'm stunned as well.

Bibliography

Acerbi, Joseph. *Travels through Sweden, Finland, and Lapland, and to the North Cape in the Years 1798 and 1799.* Vol. 2. London: Joseph Mawman, 1802.

Ackroyd, Peter. *Blake: A Biography.* New York: Knopf, 1996.

Adamnan. *Prophecies, Miracles and Visions of St. Columba (Columcille).* Translated by J. T. Fowler. London: Henry Frowde, 1895.

Adéma, Marcel. *Apollinaire.* Translated by Denise Folliot. Melbourne: William Heinemann, 1954.

Aikin, J. B. *The Christian Minstrel.* Philadelphia: T. K. Collins, 1858.

Alighieri, Dante. *The Divine Comedy of Dante Alighieri.* Vol. 1, *Inferno.* Translated by Robert M. Durling. New York: Oxford University Press, 1996.

Ambrosio, Chiara. "Cubism and the Fourth Dimension." *Interdisciplinary Science Reviews* 41, no. 2–3 (June–September 2016): 202–21.

Apollinaire, Guillaume. *Alcools suivi de Le Bestiaire et de Vitam impendere amori.* Paris: Gallimard, 1920.

———. *The Bestiary or Procession of Orpheus*. Translated by X. J. Kennedy. Baltimore: Johns Hopkins University Press, 2011.

———. *Selected Writings*. Translated by Roger Shattuck. New York: New Directions, 1971.

Aquinas, Thomas. *Sermon-Conferences of St. Thomas Aquinas on the Apostles' Creed*. Edited by Nicholas R. Ayo. Eugene, OR: Wipf & Stock, 1988.

Barfield, Owen. *Poetic Diction: A Study in Meaning*. Middletown, CT: Wesleyan University Press, 1973.

———. *The Rediscovery of Meaning and Other Essays*. Middletown, CT: Wesleyan University Press, 1977.

———. *Saving the Appearances: A Study in Idolatry*. New York: Harcourt, Brace & World, 1965.

Beattie, James. *The Poetical Works of James Beattie*. London: William Pickering, 1831.

Bentley, G. E., Jr. *The Stranger from Paradise: A Biography of William Blake*. New Haven, CT: Yale University Press, 2001.

Blake, William. *Blake: Complete Writings with Variant Readings*. Edited by Geoffrey Keynes. London: Oxford University Press, 1972.

———. *The Early Illuminated Books*. Facsimile. Edited by Morris Eaves, Robert N. Essick, and Joseph Viscomi. Princeton, NJ: The William Blake Trust/Princeton University Press, 1993.

———. *Jerusalem: The Emanation of the Giant Albion*. Facsimile. Edited by Morton D. Paley. Princeton, NJ: The William Blake Trust/Princeton University Press, 1991.

———. *The Marriage of Heaven and Hell*. Facsimile. Introduction and commentary by Sir Geoffrey Keynes. London: Oxford University Press, 1975.

———. *Milton a Poem*. Facsimile. Edited by Robert N. Essick and Joseph Viscomi. Princeton, NJ: The William Blake Trust/Princeton University Press, 1995.

———. *Poetical Sketches*. Facsimile. London: Tate Publishing, 2007.

———. *Songs of Innocence and of Experience*. Facsimile. Edited by Andrew Lincoln. Princeton, NJ: The William Blake Trust/Princeton University Press, 1991.

Bloom, Harold, and Alexis Harley, eds. *Bloom's Classic Critical Views: William Blake*. New York: Infobase Publishing, 2008.

Blyth, R. H. *Haiku*. Vol. 1, *Eastern Culture*. Tokyo: Hokuseido Press, 1949.

———. *Haiku*. Vol. 3. Tokyo: Hokuseido Press, 1950.

———. *A History of Haiku*, Vol. 1. Tokyo: Hokuseido Press, 1963.

Bohn, Willard. *Apollinaire on the Edge: Modern Art, Popular Culture, and the Avant-Garde*. Amsterdam: Rodopi, 2010.

———. "Contemplating Apollinaire's *Bestiaire*," *Modern Language Review* 99, no. 1 (January 2004): 45–51.

Boswell, James. *The Life of Samuel Johnson*. Vol. 1. London: Dent, 1906 (1791).

Bowra, C. M. *Greek Lyric Poetry from Alcman to Simonides*. Oxford: Oxford University Press, 1961.

Bradley, Ian. *Columba: Pilgrim and Penitent*. Glasgow: Wild Goose, 1996.

Burd, Henry Alfred. *Joseph Ritson: A Critical Biography*. Urbana, IL: University of Illinois Press, 1916.

Carmichael, Alexander. *Carmina Gadelica: Hymns and Incantations*. Vol. 1. Edinburgh: T&A Constable, 1900.

Cefalu, Paul. "Thomistic Metaphysics and Ethics in the Prose and Poetry of Thomas Traherne." *Literature and Theology* 16, no. 3 (September 2002): 248–69.

Chambers, R., ed. *The Book of Days: A Miscellany of Popular Antiquities*. Vol. 1. Edinburgh: W&R Chambers, 1863.

Chesterton, G. K. *Varied Types*. New York: Dodd, Mead, 1905.

Clancy, Thomas Owen, Murray Pittock, Ian Brown, and Susan Manning, eds. *The Edinburgh History of Scottish Literature*. Vol. 1, *From Columba to the Union (until 1707)*. Edinburgh: Edinburgh University Press, 2007.

Connor, Steven. *Fly*. London: Reaktion, 2006.

Corcoran, Kevin. *Rethinking Human Nature: A Christian Materialist Alternative to the Soul*. Grand Rapids, MI: Baker, 2006.

Corney, Bolton. *Curiosities of Literature by Isaac D'Israeli Illustrated*. London: Richard Bentley, 1838.

Cowley, Abraham. *Poems*. London: Humphrey Moseley, 1656.

———. *The Works of Abraham Cowley*. 5th ed. London: Henry Herringman, 1678.

Damon, S. Foster. *A Blake Dictionary: The Ideas and Symbols of William Blake*. Hanover, NH: University Press of New England, 1988.

de Gasztold, Carmen Bernos. *The Creatures' Choir*. Translated by Rumer Godden. New York: Viking, 1965.

de la Mare, Walter. *A Choice of de la Mare's Verse*. Edited by W. H. Auden. London: Faber & Faber, 1963.

Dickinson, Emily. *Emily Dickinson's Poems: As She Preserved Them*. Edited by Cristanne Miller. Cambridge, MA: Belknap Press, 2016.

———. *The Letters of Emily Dickinson*. Vol. 1. Edited by Mabel Loomis Todd. Boston: Little, Brown, 1906.

———. *The Master Letters of Emily Dickinson*. Amherst, MA: Amherst College Press, 1986.

———. *The Poems of Emily Dickinson*. Edited by Martha Dickinson Bianchi and Alfred Leete Hampson. Boston: Little, Brown, 1939.

———. *The Poems of Emily Dickinson*. Vol. 1. Edited by Thomas J. Johnson. Cambridge, MA: Belknap Press, 1963.

———. *Selected Letters*. Edited by Thomas H. Johnson. Cambridge, MA: Belknap Press, 1986.

D'Israeli, Isaac. *Curiosities of Literature*. London: George Routledge & Sons, 1866 (1791).

Dobson, Austin. *Old-World Idylls and Other Verses*. London: Kegan Paul, Trench, Trübner, 1893.

Dreamer, Percy, Ralph Vaughan Williams, and Martin Shaw, eds. *Songs of Praise*. London: Oxford University Press, 1931.

Dunlop, Eileen. *Tales of Columba*. Dublin: Poolbeg, 1992.

Ellis, Edwin J., ed. *Facsimile of the Original Outlines before Coloring of* The Songs of Innocence and of Experience *Executed by William Blake*. London: Bernard Quaritch, 1893.

Elton, Charles I. "A Relic of William Oldys." *The Cornhill Magazine*, n.s., vol. 4 (January–June 1898). London: Smith, Elder, 1898.

Emerson, Ralph Waldo. *Essays: Second Series*. Boston: James Munroe, 1844.

———. *Poems*. Boston: James Monroe, 1847.

Erdman, David V., and Donald K. Moore, eds. *The Notebook of William Blake: A Photographic and Typographic Facsimile*. London: Oxford University Press, 1973.

Farren, Robert. *The Course of Irish Verse*. New York: Sheed & Ward, 1947.

———. *Selected Poems*. London: Sheed & Ward, 1951.

———. *This Man Was Ireland: The Song of Colmcille, the Exile: A Poem*. New York: Sheed & Ward, 1943.

Folger, Tim. "Your Daily Dose of Quantum: How the Science of the Super Small Lets You Smell, See, Touch and More." *Discover* 39, no. 9 (November 2018): 30–37.

Franklin, Benjamin. *Writings: The Autobiography, Poor Richard's Almanack, Bagatelles, Pamphlets, Essays, and Letters*. New York: Library of America, 1987.

Freedman, Linda. *Emily Dickinson and the Religious Imagination*. Cambridge: Cambridge University Press, 2011.

Fry, Edward F. *Cubism*. New York: McGraw-Hill, 1966.

Gagnon, Steve. "Questions and Answers: How Much of an Atom Is Empty Space." Jefferson Lab. https://tinyurl.com/y4all9hj.

Garnett, Richard. *William Blake: Painter and Poet*. London: Seeley, 1895.

Genova, Pamela A. "The Poetics of Visual Cubism: Guillaume Apollinaire on Pablo Picasso." *Studies in Twentieth-Century Literature* 27, no. 1 (January 1, 2003).

Gilchrist, Alexander. *Life of William Blake, "Pictor Ignotus."* London: Macmillan, 1863.

Gill, Robert D. *Fly-ku! To Swat or Not to Swat*. Key Biscayne, FL: Paraverse, 2004.

Goethe, Johann Wolfgang von. *The Poems of Goethe*. Translated by Edgar Alfred Bowring. London: Parker & Son, 1853.

Habegger, Alfred. *My Wars Are Laid Away in Books: The Life of Emily Dickinson*. New York: Modern Library, 2002.

Hallo, William W., and K. Lawson Younger, eds. *The Context of Scripture: Monumental Inscriptions from the Biblical World*. Vol. 2. Leiden: Brill, 1997.

Herbert, George. *The Poems of George Herbert*. London: Oxford University Press, 1974.

Herrick, Robert. *The Poems of Robert Herrick*. London: Oxford University Press, 1933.

Hervey, James. *Meditations and Contemplations*. London: John & James Rivington, 1748.

Hobbes, Thomas. *Leviathan*. New York: Penguin, 1985 (1651).

Hofer, Philip, ed. *Eighteenth-Century Book Illustrations*. Augustan Reprint Society 58. Los Angeles: University of California, 1956.

Hooke, Robert. *Micrographia: Or Some Physiological Descriptions of Minute Bodies Made by Magnifying Glasses with Observations and Inquiries Thereupon*. London: The Royal Society of London, 1665.

Issa, Kobayashi. *The Autumn Wind: A Selection from the Poems of Issa*. Translated by Lewis Mackenzie. Tokyo: Kondansha International, 1984.

———. *Cup of Tea Poems: Selected Haiku of Kobayashi Issa*. Translated by David G. Lanoue. Berkeley, CA: Asian Humanities Press, 1991.

———. *The Dumpling Field: Haiku of Issa*. Translated by Lucien Stryk and Noboru Fujiwara. Athens: Swallow Press/Ohio University Press, 1991.

———. *A Few Flies and I: Haiku by Issa*. Translated by R. H. Blyth and Nobuyuki Yuasa. New York: Random House, 1969.

———. *The Spring of My Life and Selected Haiku*. Translated by Sam Hamill. Boston: Shambhala, 1997.

———. *Ten Poems by Issa: English Versions by Robert Bly*. Edited by Robert Bly. Illustrated by Arthur Okamura. Point Reyes Station, CA: Floating Island, 1992.

———. *En village de miséreux: Choix de poèmes*. Translated into French by Jean Cholley. Paris: Gallimard, 1996.

Johnson, Samuel. *The Latin Poems*. Edited by Niall Rudd. Lewisburg, PA: Bucknell University Press, 2005.

Kolocotroni, Vassiliki, Jane Goldman, and Olga Taxidou, eds. *Modernism: An Anthology of Sources and Documents*. Chicago: University of Chicago Press, 1998.

Kwazny, Melizza, ed. *Toward the Open Field: Poets on the Art of Poetry, 1800–1950*. Middletown, CT: Wesleyan University Press, 2003.

La Fontaine, Jean de. *The Fables of La Fontaine*. Translated by E. Wright. London: Ingram, Cooke, 1853.

Lanoue, David G. *Pure Land Haiku: The Art of Priest Issa*. Reno, NV: Buddhist Books International, 2004.

L'Estrange, Roger, ed. *Seneca's Morals by Way of Abstract*. Edinburgh: Martin & Sons, 1776.

Lewis, C. S. *The Collected Letters of C. S. Lewis*. Vol. 2, *Books, Broadcasts, and the War, 1931–1949*. Edited by Walter Hooper. New York: HarperCollins, 2004.

———. *Surprised by Joy*. New York: Harcourt, Brace & World, 1955.

Linceus, Galileus Galieus. *The Systeme of the World: In Four Dialogues—Wherein the Two Grand Systemes of Ptolemy and Copernicus Are Largely Discoursed of . . . Inglished from the Original Italian by Thomas Salusbury*. London: William Leybourne, 1661.

Lindsay, Vachel. *The Congo and Other Poems*. New York: Macmillan, 1915.

Little, Roger. *Guillaume Apollinaire*. London: Athlone Press, 1976.

Lonsdale, Roger, ed. *The New Oxford Book of Eighteenth Century Verse*. Oxford: Oxford University Press, 1984.

Lucian. *Lucian*. Translated by A. M. Harmon. London: William Heinemann, 1913.

———. *The Works of Lucian of Samosata*. Translated by H. W. Fowler and F. G. Fowler. Adelaide: University of Adelaide, 2014. https://tinyurl.com/yygxuekk.

MacDonagh, Donagh, and Lennox Robinson, eds. *The Oxford Book of Irish Verse: XVIIth Century–XXth Century*. London: Oxford University Press, 1978.

Mackay, Charles. *Songs of England*. London: Houlston & Wright, n.d.

McClintock, Mike. *A Fly Went By*. Illustrated by Fritz Siebel. New York: Random House, 1958.

McGann, Jerome J., ed. *The New Oxford Book of Romantic Period Verse*. Oxford: Oxford University Press, 1993.

McIntosh, James. *Nimble Believing: Dickinson and the Unknown.* Ann Arbor, MI: University of Michigan Press, 2000.

Merton, Thomas. *The Road to Joy: Letters to New and Old Friends.* Edited by Robert E. Daggy. New York: Farrar, Straus & Giroux, 1989.

Milosz, Czeslaw. *Second Space: New Poems.* Translated by Czeslaw Milosz and Robert Haas. New York: HarperCollins, 2004.

Muggeridge, Malcolm. *The Third Testament.* Boston: Little, Brown, 1976.

Murphy, Kathryn. "Thomas Traherne, Thomas Hobbes, and the Rhetoric of Realism." *The Seventeenth Century* 28, no. 4 (2013): 419–39.

O'Donnell, Manus. *Betha Colaim Chille: Life of Columcille.* Translated by A. O'Kelleher and G. Schoepperle. Urbana, IL: University of Illinois, 1918.

Oldys, William. *A Collection of Epigrams, to Which Is Prefixed a Critical Dissertation on This Species of Poetry.* London: J. Walthoe, 1727.

———. *A Dissertation upon Pamphlets: In a Letter to a Nobleman.* London: 1731.

Olsen, Kirstin. *Daily Life in 18th-Century England.* 2nd ed. Santa Barbara, CA: Greenwood, 2017.

Page, Nick. *Lord Minimus: The Extraordinary Life of Britain's Smallest Man.* New York: St. Martin's, 2002.

Park, Edwards A., Austin Phelps, and Lowell Mason, eds. *The Sabbath Hymn Book for the Service of Song in the House of the Lord.* New York: Mason Brothers, 1858.

Peacock, W., ed. *English Verse.* Vol. 2, *Campion to the Ballads.* London: Oxford University Press, 1971.

———. *English Verse.* Vol. 3, *Dryden to Wordsworth.* London: Oxford University Press, 1972.

Phillips, Michael. *William Blake: The Creation of the* Songs *from Manuscript to Illuminated Printing.* Princeton, NJ: Princeton University Press, 2000.

Picasso, Pablo. "Picasso Speaks." In *The Arts.* New York: The Arts Publishing Corporation, 1923.

Raine, Kathleen. *Golgonooza City of Imagination: Last Studies in William Blake.* Hudson, NY: Lindisfarne Press, 1991.

———. *William Blake*. London: Thames & Hudson, 1970.

Reid, Thomas Wilson, et al., eds. *The Book of the Cheese, Being Traits and Stories of "Ye Olde Cheddar Cheese."* London: Ye Olde Cheddar Cheese, 1937.

Rimmer, Alfred. *Ancient Stone Crosses of England*. London: Virtue, Spaulding, 1875.

Ritson, Joseph, ed. *Robin Hood: A Collection of All the Ancient Poems, Songs, and Ballads, Now Extant, Relative to that Celebrated English Outlaw: To Which Are Prefixed Historical Anecdotes of His Life.* 2 vols. London: T. Egerton, 1795.

———, ed. *Select Collection of English Songs in Three Volumes, Volume the Second*. London: J. Johnson in St. Paul's Churchyard, 1783.

Rovelli, Carlo. *Seven Brief Lessons on Physics*. New York: Riverhead, 2016.

Salter, K. W. *Thomas Traherne: Mystic and Poet*. New York: Barnes & Noble, 1965.

Sánchez-Bayo, Francisco, and Kris A. G. Wyckhuys. "Worldwide Decline of Entomofauna: A Review of Its Drivers." *Biological Conservation* 232 (April 2019): 8–27. doi.org/10.1016/j.biocon.2019.01.020.

Sartre, Jean-Paul. *No Exit and Three Other Plays*. New York: Vintage, 1958.

The Scarborough Miscellany for the Year 1732, Consisting of Original Poems, Tales, Songs, Epigrams, etc. London: J. Roberts, 1732.

Seneca. *Moral Essays*. Vol. 2. Loeb Classical Library. Cambridge, MA: Harvard University Press, 1990.

Shakespeare, William. *Titus Andronicus*. The Arden Shakespeare. London: Methuen, 1961.

———. *The Arden Shakespeare*. 39 vols. London: Methuen, 1899–1924.

Stanley, Thomas. *Anacreon, Bion, and Moschus with Other Translations*. London: Longman, Hurst, Rees, Orme & Brown, 1815 (1651).

Stein, Gertrude. *Geography and Plays*. Boston: Four Seas, 1922.

Swedenborg, Emanuel. *The Wisdom of Angels Concerning Divine Love and Divine Wisdom*. Translated by Nathaniel Tucker. London: W. Chalklen, 1788.

Thompson, E. P. *Witness against the Beast: William Blake and the Moral Law*. New York: The New Press, 1993.

Tilton, Theodore. *The Sexton's Tale and Other Poems*. New York: Sheldon, 1867.

Tolkien, J. R. R. *The Monsters and the Critics and Other Essays*. Boston: Houghton Mifflin, 1983.

Townsend-Hudson, Shelley. *When I Got Drunk with My Mother*. Ada, MI: Perkipery, 2019.

Traherne, Thomas. *The Golden Age of Spiritual Writing: Thomas Traherne: Poetry and Prose*. Edited by Denise Inge. London: SPCK, 2002.

———. *The Works of Thomas Traherne*. Vol. 1, *Inducements to Retirednes, A Sober View of Dr. Twisses his Considerations, Seeds of Eternity of the Nature of the Soul, The Kingdom of God*. Edited by Jan Ross. Cambridge, MA: D. S. Brewer, 2005.

———. *The Works of Thomas Traherne*. Vol 2, *Commentaries of Heaven, Part 1: Abhorrence to Alone*. Edited by Jan Ross. Cambridge, MA: D. S. Brewer, 2007.

———. *The Works of Thomas Traherne*. Vol. 3, *Commentaries of Heaven, Part 2: Al-Sufficient to Bastard*. Edited by Jan Ross. Cambridge, MA: D. S. Brewer, 2007.

———. *The Works of Thomas Traherne*. Vol. 5, *Centuries of Meditations and Select Meditations*. Edited by Jan Ross. Cambridge, MA: D. S. Brewer, 2013.

———. *The Works of Thomas Traherne*. Vol. 6, *Poems from the Dobell Folio, Poems of Felicity, The Ceremonial Law, Poems from the Early Notebook*. Edited by Jan Ross. Cambridge, MA: D. S. Brewer, 2014.

Turner, Charles Tennyson. *Collected Sonnets Old and New*. London: C. Kegan Paul, 1880.

Tyson, Gerald P. *Joseph Johnson: A Liberal Publisher*. Iowa City: University of Iowa Press, 1979.

Ueda, Makoto. *Dew on the Grass: The Life and Poetry of Kobayashi Issa*. Boston: Brill, 2004.

Untermeyer, Louis. *Lives of the Poets: The Story of One Thousand Years of English and American Poetry*. New York: Simon & Schuster, 1959.

Viscomi, Joseph. *Blake and the Idea of the Book*. Princeton, NJ: Princeton University Press, 1993.

Waddell, Helen. *Beasts and Saints*. Grand Rapids, MI: Eerdmans, 1995.

Wade, Gladys I. "St. Thomas Aquinas and Thomas Traherne." *New Blackfriars* 12, no. 140 (November 1931): 666–73.

———. *Thomas Traherne*. Princeton, NJ: Princeton University Press, 1944.

West, M. L., trans. *Greek Lyric Poetry*. Oxford: Oxford University Press, 1993.

Whitman, Walt. *Poetry and Prose*. New York: Library of America, 1982.

———. *Walt Whitman Speaks*. Edited by Brenda Wineapple. New York: Library of America, 2019.

Willis, Francis. *Anacreon Done into English Out of the Original Greek*. Oxford: 1683.

Yeowell, James, and William Oldys. *A Literary Antiquary: Memoir of William Oldys, Esq., . . . Together with His Diary, Choice Notes from His Adversaria, and an Account of the London Libraries*. London: Spottiswoode, 1862.

Yong, Ed. "Is the Insect Apocalypse Really Upon Us?" *The Atlantic*, February 19, 2019. https://tinyurl.com/y6jnrxd9.

Yuasa, Nobuyuki, trans. *The Year of My Life: A Translation of Issa's* Oraga Haru. 2nd ed. Berkeley, CA: University of California Press, 1972.